THE
ROYAL TOUR
—— 1901 ——

Harry Price in the uniform of an Able Seaman at the turn of the century

THE
ROYAL TOUR
— 1901 —

OR THE CRUISE OF
H.M.S. OPHIR

*BEING A LOWER DECK ACCOUNT OF THEIR
ROYAL HIGHNESSES, THE DUKE AND DUCHESS OF CORNWALL AND YORK'S
VOYAGE AROUND THE BRITISH EMPIRE*

Petty Officer HARRY PRICE

Webb&Bower
EXETER, ENGLAND

First published in Great Britain 1980 by
Webb & Bower (Publishers) Limited,
33 Southernhay East, Exeter, Devon, EX1 1NS

Distributed by WHS Distributors
(a division of W.H. Smith and Son Limited)
St John's House, East Street,
Leicester, LE1 6NE

British Library Cataloguing in Publication Data

Price, Harry, *b. 1877*
  The Royal Tour, 1901, or, The cruise of H.M.S.
'Ophir'.
  1. George V *King of Great Britain*
  2. Mary, *Queen, consort of George V, King of Great
  Britain* 3. Visits of state – Commonwealth of
  Nations 4. Manuscripts, English – Facsimiles
  5. Great Britain – Kings and rulers – Biography
  I. Title
  910'.09171'241   DA573

  ISBN 0-906671-10-8

Printed and bound in Italy by Arnoldo Mondadori Editore

HARRY PRICE 1877–1965

Harry Price was born in Birmingham in 1877. His parents came from Welsh families who had emigrated from their country to the expanding industrial city of Birmingham, where his father became a master builder. The family produced several "romantics", at least one of whom became a minor poet and another, Harry's brother, a Royal Academician. Many were skilled anglers and having settled in Birmingham were obliged to change from game to coarse fishing. In the latter field they eventually became the "champion fishing family of Birmingham".

Harry's artistic ability was noted by his schoolmaster and he was sent to the Birmingham School of Art, where in a couple of weeks he progressed right through the School, from bottom to top class. He was then told that he had such natural talent that they couldn't teach him anything. This only added to his growing dislike of Birmingham, "the land of bricks and mortar," so he left home in 1893 and joined the Royal Navy as a Boy. Except to attend his mother's funeral he never returned.

Stationed at Devonport he found the fulfilment of his subconscious longings on his door-step in the countryside of Devon and Cornwall. On his leaves and any free time he walked for miles along the Cornish coastal footpaths and over Dartmoor, and in later life often remembered that the sight of a young sailor walking for pleasure before the turn of the century aroused much interest.

Dartmoor was the main attraction, and one of his favourite excursions was diagonally across the moor from Plymouth to the Chagford area. He always travelled light, with little or no money but with a little fishing tackle and painting materials. Thus he could always catch food – he was an expert at cooking fish on the river bank – and earn his keep by painting. Eventually he found Fingle Gorge (he never travelled with a map) and the account of his discovery of Fingle Bridge and Drewsteignton is most moving. He wept on arrival at the bridge over the River Teign and the Church bells seemed to welcome him at Drewsteignton where he went to morning service, and he silently vowed that this was where he would make his home when he left the Navy. Those same bells were to ring specially for him over twenty years later when he made a triumphant return to his "home" village after distinguished service in the Great War. Although he travelled virtually all over the world in the course of his service life, he remained true to this vow and still declared that nowhere in the world was more attractive to him.

Although he was a loyal and true patriot he joined the Navy "to see the world" rather than to serve his country and he often rebelled against naval discipline, as his service record shows. He once led a minor mutiny but was pardoned because he was also responsible for ending it, when it began to reach ugly proportions.

In 1899 he joined the *Britannia*, the senior of two training ships moored in the river Dart, which were the forerunners of the present Royal Naval College at Dartmouth. On this ship his good record and rapid promotion probably led to his being chosen as a member of the crew of the *Ophir* for the Royal Tour of 1901. He served on that ship from February to November 1901. On leaving the Royal Navy in 1907 he joined the Royal Fleet Reserve and was called up for service in the Great War on 2nd August, 1914.

During that war he served in five ships, three of which were sunk within the space of nine months. These included the *Ocean* and the *Majestic* and from the former he was picked up by destroyer after fourteen hours in the water. He was a superb natural swimmer and, being born with a caul, always declared: "I could never drown." He was demobilized in March 1919 after he had been awarded the Distinguished Service Medal for his services.

For an ordinary seaman he made his service career a very colourful one, for besides the Royal Tour he travelled extensively and grasped every opportunity to see the world. He even lived for a short while with cowboys in Texas after he had passed their test of outdrinking them in a saloon bar in Houston, and he spent a short time in an Indian Reserve in North America where he painted designs and emblems on wigwams.

After settling in Drewsteignton he declared: "I had no wish to wander any more – only up and down the banks of the river Teign, fishing for salmon and trout." He was a talented naturalist and made a fine collection of butterflies and birds' eggs. Because of this and his ability to climb well he worked for a while as a free-lance egg collector for Watkins and Doncaster of the Strand, London. This led, in turn, to an association with Richard Kearton, the pioneer bird photographer, and thus he experienced the transition from egg collecting to bird photography.

On the river Teign he quickly adapted his coarse fishing knowledge to game fishing – the reverse of his Birmingham forbears – and in a few years became the finest angler on the river (his fishing diaries, covering about forty years, make very interesting and informative reading). He was still able to practise coarse fishing, however, at a famous local carp pool and one of the best known books on carp fishing is largely about his escapades there, although the identity of the man and the pool are disguised. He also became an expert gardener and his produce sometimes went to the Royal Horticultural Society's shows in London, as non-competitive exhibits. In his later years he grew all his own tobacco – he was a moderately heavy pipe smoker – and cured it by a method based on his knowledge of what he had seen in the tobacco industries of Havana and Rhodesia.

All the while he painted, mainly in oils, and made a number of interesting models, when he had time and "when the spirit moves me". Perhaps his greatest work is a model of his first ship, HMS *Impregnable*, a fully rigged three-decker, which off and on took about seven years to complete. His most ingenious model was of the ship in which he used to smuggle tobacco out of the dockyard. In addition he took up wood carving when he was well over seventy years of age and after a five-year disability, following a stroke at the age of eighty-three, he was still making simple sketches as he lay in his hospital bed up to the time that he died in June 1965, at the age of eighty-eight.

JACK PRICE
Fingle Bridge, Devon

Conduct.

Name *Harry Price*

Second Class for Conduct
inclusive dates

From	To	Character	Ability in Rating, noting substantive rating in brackets	Whole R.M.G.	Date	Captain's Signature
		V.g			8 Dec 94	
		V.g			5 Feb 95	
		V.g			31 Dec 95	
		Good			31 Dec 96	
		V.g			31 Dec 97	
		V.g			31 Dec 98	
		V.g			31 Dec 99	
		V.g			31 Dec 00	
		V.g			31 Dec 01	
		V.g			31 Dec 02	
		V.g			31 Dec 03	
		Good			31 Dec 04	
		V.g			31 Dec 05	
		V.g			31 Dec 06	
		V.g			8 Feb 07	

Good Conduct Badges

Date	1st, 2nd, 3rd	Granted, Deprived, Restored					
1 Jan 99	1st	Granted	V.g		31 Dec 13	
12 Feb 03	2nd	Granted	V.g	Sat	31 Dec 14	
27 Feb 04	2nd	Deprived	Good	Supt	31 Dec 15	
28 Apl 04	1st	Deprived	V.g	Sat	31 Dec 16	
20 Apl 05	1st	Restored	V.g	Supt	31 Dec 17	
19 Oct 05	2nd	Restored	V.g	Supr	31 Dec 18	
9 Feb 15	2nd	Deprived	V.g		28 Mobilsg	
10 Aug 15	2nd	Restored				
10 Aug 17	3rd	Granted				

	Date	F.P. or W.T.	Days	Date	F.P. or W.T.	Days	Date	F.P. or W.T.	Days	Date	F.P. or W.T.	Days
Time Forfeited	9 Oct 96	C	6									

The corner of this Certificate is to be cut off if the man is discharged with a "Bad" character or with disgrace, or if specially directed by the Admiralty. If the corner is cut off, the fact is to be noted in the Ledger.

True copy from Admiralty Records.

CERTIFICATE of the Service of

Harry Price in the Royal Navy.

Port Division	*Devonport*	Official Number	174,854.

Date of Birth 6 February 1877

Nearest known Relative or Friend. (Relationship, Name, and Address)

Where born: Parish *Birmingham*; Town or County *Warwick*

Usual place of Residence

Trade brought up to *Painter & Decorator*

Religious Denomination

Can Swim

Man's signature on discharge to pension {

Continuous Service and Special Service Engagements
(This space should be used by the man of Non-C.S. men, to note the term on which he receives a free issue of Bedding or Bedding Gratuities)

Date of actually volunteering	Commencement of time	Period volunteered for	Date received or forfeited	Nature of Decoration
27 July 1893	6 Feb 95	12 years	March 24 5 1919	Distinguished Service Med.
			12 APR 1922	1914-15 Star, British War Medal, Victory Medal

Medals, Clasps, &c.

Description of Person	Stature		Chest, In.	Colour of			Marks, Wounds, and Scars
	Feet	In.		Hair	Eyes	Complexion	
On Entry as a Boy	5	4½		Lt Brn	Blue	Fresh	Clasped hands, heart & anchor on Lt. forearm
On advancement to man's rating, or on entry under 28 years	5	7		Brown			
On re-entry for C.S. or for Non-C.S. after attaining 28 years							
Further description if necessary							

N. 42716/15.
Sta. 303/16.
Sta. 23/18.

2.

Name *Harry Price*

Ship's Name	List and No.	Rating	From	To	Cause of Discharge
Impregnable	15	6163	Boy II	27 July 93	5 Sep 94	
	"		Boy I	6 Sep 94	3 Dec 94	
Colossus	16	317	"	4 Dec 94	13 Dec 94	
Vivid	15²	3518	"	14 Dec 94	17 Dec 94	
Trafalgar	5	424	"	18 Dec 94	5 Feb 95	
	"		Ord Smn	6 Feb 95	28 Mch 96	
Cruiser	16	877	"	24 Mch 96	31 Aug 96	
Trafalgar	5	185	A.B	1 Sep 96	11 Sep 97	
Royal Sovereign	5	133	"	12 Sep 97	3 Feb 98	
Vivid I	15t	1425	"	4 Feb 98	19 Apl 98	
Cambridge	15	5628	"	20 Apl 98	22 Oct 98	
Defiance	14	2112	"	23 Oct 98	25 Feb 99	
Vivid I	15²	5423	"	26 Feb 99	1 May 99	
Britannia	5	93	"	2 May 99	25 May 00	
	"		Ldg Smn	26 May 00	28 Jan 01	
	"		P.O II	29 Jan 01	21 Feb 01	
Vivid I	15	4435	"	21 Feb 01	25 Feb 01	
Ophir	5	97	"	26 Feb 01	6 Nov 01	
Vivid	15'	4942	"	7 Nov 01	1 Feb 02	
Cambridge	15	4835	"	2 Feb 02	3 Feb 02	
Defiance	14	3534	"	4 Feb 02	5 Apl 02	
Vivid	15'	630	"	6 Apl 02	4 June 02	
Ariadne	5	16	"	5 June 02	8 July 03	
Warrior	12²	2	"	1 July 03	11 Aug 03	
Vivid I	15'	2450	"	12 Aug 03	4 Nov 03	
Donegal	5	68	"	5 Nov 03	5 Feb 04	
	"		Ldg Smn	6 Feb 04	19 Apl 04	

Date	Wounds received in Action and Hurt Certificate; also any meritorious Service, Special recommendations, Prize or other Grants	Captain's Signature
3-11-20	Paid £12-10 s. d. Naval Prize Fund.	
14 OCT 1922	Final Share of Naval Prize Fund Paid	
26 OCT 1926	Supplementary Prize Share Paid.	

---

3. Service.

Ship's Name	List and No.	Rating	From	To	Cause of Discharge
Donegal	5	68	A.B	20 Apl 04	6 Jan 05	
Vivid I	15²	14940	"	7 Jan 05	18 Feb 05	
Defiance	14	6356	"	19 Feb 05	20 May 05	
Vivid	15²	17170	"	21 May 05	10 July 05	
New Zealand	5	256	"	11 July 05	12 Jan 07	
Vivid I	15²	5696	"	13 Jan 07	8 Feb 07	Shore C.S.expired
Joined R.F.R. Devonport 13.1754 9 February 1907					
Re-engrolled 9 February 1912 to serve to 8 February 1917 (ST)					
Ocean	5	101	A.B	2 Aug 14	18 Mch 15	
Majestic	14	206	"	19 Mch 15	27 May 15	
Vivid I	15²	531	"	28 May 15	9 July 15	
Defiance	14	202	"	10 July 15	13 Sep 15	
Liverpool	5²	2	"	14 Sep 15	28 Mch 19	demobilised

Awarded R.F.R. Gratuity of £50 Mar 18
Awarded R.F.R. Add gral of £50 Oct 20

Date	Particulars	Captain's Signature	Date	Particulars	Captain's Signature

---

The certificate of the service of Harry Price in the Royal Navy 1893-1919

THE "ROYAL TOUR"

OR THE CRUISE
OF
"H.M.S. OPHIR"

BEING A LOWER DECK ACCOUNT, OF THEIR "ROYAL HIGHNESSES, THE DUKE AND DUCHESS OF CORNWALL AND YORK'S, VOYAGE AROUND THE BRITISH EMPIRE.

1901

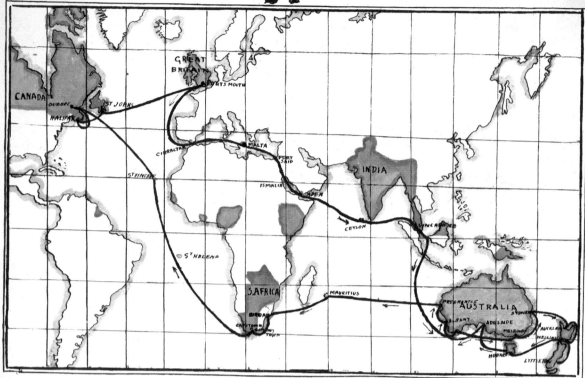

 Chart showing line of route, distance covered about 40,000 Mls

NAME OF PLACE	DATE OF ARRIVAL	DATE OF DEPARTURE	NAME OF PLACE	DATE OF ARRIVAL	DATE OF DEPARTURE
Portsmouth		16th Mch	Auckland	11th June	16th June
Gibraltar	20th Mch	22nd Mch	Wellington	17th "	21st "
Malta	25th Mch	27th Mch	Lyttleton	22nd "	24th "
Port Said	30th Mch	31st Mch	Hobart	2nd July	6th July
Suez	1st Apr	1st Apr	Adelaide	8th "	15th "
Aden	5th "	5th "	Albany	20th "	22nd "
Colombo	12th "	16th "	Freemantle	23rd "	26th "
Singapore	21st "	23rd "	Mauritious	4th Aug	8th Aug
Albany	3rd May	4th May	Durban	13th "	15th "
Melbourne	6th "	18th "	Simonstown	18th "	23rd "
Sydney	20th "	24th "	St Vincent	3rd Sept	5th Sep
Hawkesbury Riv	24th "	27th "	Quebec	15th "	27th "
Sydney	27th "	6th June	Halifax	23rd Sept	27th Oct
			St Johns	23rd Oct	25th "

"H.M.S. OPHIR"

OUTWARD · BOUND.

"H.M.S. DIADEM."   OUR · FIRST · ESCORT   "H.M.S. NIOBE"

Discription of the Ophir.

The leading particulars. are. length over all 482ft. beam 52ft 6in. depth 37ft.) gross register 6910 tns.) Horse power 10.000. (engines. two. independant triple ex (boilers. seven)(working pressure 160 lbs)(speed 18. knots.)

Commisioned at Tilbury docks 26 feb/01, with a compliment of 125 bluejackets, 100 marines, 37 bandsmen, 20 boys, 7 engineer officers, 88 stokers, 2 pursers, 50 stewards, 9 cooks & assistant cooks, 3 bakers, 2 butchers, 1 laundry man. and wife, 1 printer, 2 barbers, The whole under the command of Commodore A.L.Winsloe. and 21 other officers. to take "H.R.H. the Duke. and Duchess of Cornwall & York," on their colonial tour. The ships compliment with the royal suite included would be about 525 all told.

Left Tilbury docks the 27 of Febuary 1901 & ajusted compasses off "Sheerness," We then proceeded to "Portsmouth;" arriving there the following morning, and anchored at "Spithead" in thick fog; which delayed our going up harbour; which we did about midday; and went alongside the south railway, or farewell jetty as it is called, and in the afternoon prepared for coaling, the next day we took in several hundreds of tons. of best hand picked coal. Two remarkable features of the coaling was first the absence of dirt and dust greatley due to the manner in which the ship was protected by coaling screens; and secondly the we where coaled. by people from shore; the likes of which I had never seen done in home waters before. The next day we started taking in government stores. Nothing happened concerning us until the 8th of March when we witnessed the departure of our escort the "Snt George & Juno." for "Suez" the first named having on board two royal steam barges; On the 11th the royal yatch "Victoria & Albert" was berthed alongside the jetty astern of us. The day following was visited by "Lord Selborne" first lord of the admiralty, 15th "The King. Queen. Duke. Dutchess." ect arrived. The next day the "King" confered the "Victorian Order" on the men belonging to the guard of honour that rendered such valuable assistance. at "Windsor" at the time of the burial of our late beloved "Queen Victoria"; after which he distributed medals to men from "S. Africa". "The King" then came on board and inspected us. and then lunched with the "Duke & Duchess. Commodore". ect. About 4.30 in the evening we cast off from the jetty and proceeded slowly down the harbour, preceeded first by the "Trinity House yacht" and next by the "Alberta" with the "King and Queen" on board; eight torpedo boat destroyers in two lines one off each quarter brought up the rear; immence crowds of people lined the shores on both sides, and one could see handkerchiefs waving as far as the eye could reach, whilst several bands could be heard playing; and above all the cheers of the multitude both on shore and on the many boats which accompanied us out of the harbour. The "Alberta" still kept right ahead, till well out at "Spithead"; when she slowed down and dropped abrest of us. We then manned the rigging; and the commander. called for three cheers for the "King & Queen" which where heartily given, the "Duke. & Duchess" on the fore bridge waving. adieu he with cap; she with handkerchief. The "Alberta's" crew then gave us us three cheers, We then gave three more cheers, went full speed ahead and we soon left the "Alberta" far astern. Our first escort the "Diadem & Niobe". then took up their positions one off each quarter; and we proceeded down channel, en-route for "Gibralta." When we got fairly out at sea, the sea proved to be very moderate, only a gentle heaving of the ship to remind you that you where at sea. The next day Sunday a little rain fell, and we went to church in the Royal dining saloon, a magnificently decorated apartment the Duke was there, but the Duchess did not make her appearance; in fact nothing had been seen of her since the evening before. after divine service we where served out with a little souvenir! a small testament; with a print of the "Duke & Duchess" & children for a front ispiece; about 4 O.Clock in the evening the Duchess sent a box of shamrock on the mens messdeck with her compliments, and being the 17 of old "Ireland" everyman went to evening quarters with a spray in his cap. All went well the next day untill about 10 O.Clock in the first watch when the wind began to blow. and the sea to rise; and by midnight it was blowing half a gale, and we where tumbling about in a heavy sea, one of the hydraulic cranes got adrift and smashed our upper fore and aft bridge; we shipped large quantities of water but taking her all together the "Ophir" proved a good sea boat. The landlubbers had a very bad time and swore they would go back home when they reached Gib; but the sea moderated a good deal by the following evening, and the Duchess came on deck; the first we had seen of her since we started. The next morning we sighted the Rock; and as we got closer we saw that the whole of the channel fleet was drawn up in two lines. manned & dressed. When about ¼ a mile off the Majestic started to salute followed by the whole squadron it was a grand sight; and as we passed between the lines each ships company gave us three ringing cheers; and their bands played the King. We dropped anchor inside the **Mole** and got out the royal pulling barge, and two steam cutters. Between our ship and the landing place; was stretched two lines of 12 oared cutters. At noon the Duke left the ship in the royal barge, and she looked very nice as she passed between the lines of cutters their crews standing bare headed each officer saluting; soon after his return to the ship in the evening the whole fleet illuminated; and I only make a poor show of it in the picture below.

Channel Fleet at Gibralta

The Duke went ashore again the following day, and in the evening the fleet again illuminated the rock itself was illuminated; also the Portuguese warship, Sᵐ Gabriel but the Spanish ship Infanta ISABEL, took no part whatever in the celebrations; we prepared for sea. The next morning turned out nice and fine, and at half past nine we got up anchor], and proceeded out of harbour, and it made one feel proud to belong to such a nation as we steamed slowly through the stately lines of flag bedecked warships, and cheer after cheer echoed across the sunlit waters.

SAN.GABRIEL
PORTUGUESE

INFANTA ISABEL
SPANISH

The Magnificent again started to salute, the remainder following suit, after which we turned our ships head for Malta, signalled down the engine room for full speed, and with our second escort the Andromeda & Diana following in our wake; soon left the historic rock far behind, we then signalled for our escort to go on ahead. The day turned out to be the finest we had had since we left England and by midday it was quite hot. The following day we left off gurnseys and wore white capcovers. On our Starboard beam the coast of Africa showed up quite plain., Sunday morning we sighted the Thetis British cruiser and she signaled Bothers conditions of surrender. We went to Church in the Royal Saloon again; and the service went off much better but the Duchess was still unable to attend, in the evening we slowed down. Monday morn early we sighted Malta; and before long we perceived a number of craft approaching, which proved to be destroyers painted white; and they made a splendid spectacle as they bounded over the dark blue waters, thundering out a royal salute with their 12 ᵖᵈʳˢ as the came on in two lines in an opposite direction to us, one line passing down each side of us, and they put one in mind of a shoal of porpoises, as they left and plunged through the water; when they got astern they altered course 16 points and again passed us, and took up their positions one of each bow and in this formation we entered the harbour. The noise now became deffening as over forty men-of-war began to salute; { its puts me in mind of Parde burg} I heard a man say, a man who had served with the Naval Brigade in S. Africa. The shore from the beach to the top of the bastions was thronged with the teeming population both of Malta & Goza, and cheer after cheer reechoed from height to height. It was a splendid welcome and showed that the Maltese are quite happy under the Union Jack. We made fast head and stern to two buoys in the center of the Grand Harbour; and the water police had their work cut out to keep back the hundreds of boats or Dycoes as they are commonly called here. The "Duke & Duchess" went ashore in the royal pulling barge about midday. The shore being lined with soldiers, The Navy being stationed from the "Opera house" in "Strada Reale" to Spencers Monument

DESTROYERS ESCORTING US INTO MALTA HARBOUR

The whole fleet again saluted during the passage ashore. When their Royal Highnesses landed they looked as happy as possible, and beaming over with good humour and smiles, graciously returned the salutations of the people, and all along the route nothing but happy and joyous faces, stretched forward to catch a glimse of the illustrious son of Our King. Floriana of course was a foretaste of the reception in Valletta the houses and streets being decorated in handsome style. We all know that Valletta redily adapts itself to decoration, there is a quaintness and old time feeling about the houses, which modern cities never offer. Even without decoration Valletta is quaint picturesque and romantic, but when to its usual charms are added decorated and ever greened venetian masts, banners and flags by the hundreds flying in the breeze, beautiful triumphal arches, pavements thronged with a loyal picturesque and enthusiastic crowd, the road way lined with soldiers in Karki and Bluejackets in straw hats, and last but not least, the balconies and windows filled with visions of feminine beauty and loveliness, the world-famed Strada Reale presents a scene which no other town in Europe can furnish. Their Royal Highnesses visited the palace and inspected the guard of honour there, afterwards proceeded up to the Royal Balcony facing the mainguard, to witness the forces detailed from the Navy & Army to march past. Upwards of 6000 men defiled past the Royal Balcony in gallant style. The march past over their Royal Highnesses lunched with His Excellency the governor at the Palace, their Royal Highnesses subsiquently returned to the Ophir about midnight. 27th of March the day of departure was a very event full one, and even early in the morning, one could see preperations going on and as the evening drew on, weird looking craft began to make their appearence on the water, most of them resembling animals & birds, the best products being a swan & whale, the Elephant Crocodile Seaserpert Lion Camel & Drayon being very good; At eight p.m. as by magic the whole fleet illuminated

Aquatic
Display at
Malta

and in the background 500 starrockets ascended simultaniously; the harbour now presented a sight the likes of which I had never seen before

All round the harbour coloured lamps could be seen outlining the old battlements and bastions, whilst along the sea front the Maltese had made a grand show every window door gable ect being festuned with coloured lamps, but it was on the water that all eyes where fixed; apart from the fleet the Ophir was also illuminated and the weird craft; the dragons, & sea serpent kept up a continous rain of fire and smoke from their mouths in the shape of all manner of fireworks, Lined up along side both sides of the harbour, outside the fleet where the destroyers, their searchlights crossing over us, and making an arch

H.M.S ANDROMEDA.   H.M.S. DIANA.

way reaching to the sky. About half past nine another flight of 500 rockets ascended, and at midnight a grand salvo of a thousand rockets was the signal for us to depart. As we slipped the buoy, the forts began to salute, and all the steamers kept up a continual din with their hooters And as we slowly passed down the harbour between the thousands of boats the ones on the starboard hand burnt green port fires, and on the port side they used red ones, whilst the people cheered them selves hoarse

·······«««⟨ MALTA'S SONG OF WELCOME ⟩»»»·······

THEY COME, OUR HOPE FROM ALBIONS SHORES AFAR,
TO NAME OF AGE A RACE NEATH SOUTHERN STAR;
AND NATIONS, ENVIOUS, MARK THEIR STEEL CLAD TRAIN,
STRETCHING, IMPERIOUS, LEAGUES ACROSS THE MAIN.
BUT LO! WE HAIL THE LAND WITH PROMISE GREAT
SELF-STRONG PROCLAIMED WITH POMP BY PARENT STATE
AND VITAL ORGAN OF THE EMPIRE'S HEART
IN GREATNESS GROWN WITH EACH EXPANDING PART.
LOUD IN AUSTRALIA'S JOY, WITH HEART AND VOICE
TO ALL THE WORLD, WE CRY, THAT WE REJOICE

THEN DECK THE TOWN OF LA VALLETTE,
WITH FLAG, AND FLOWER, AND FAIRY LAMP.
LET JOYOUS HEARTS NEW JOY BEGET
WITH HUM OF THRONG, AND MARTIAL TRAMP
AT SIGHT OF GLIDING CARNIVAL
OF CRAFT WEIRD BRIGHT FANTASTICAL
AT SHOWER OF STARS OF PAINTED LIGHT, AT MUSIC'S THRILL, AT CANNON'S ROAR
REECHOING FROM THE BASTIONED HEIGHT THAT SPURNED THE TURK FROM MALTA'S SHORE

MALTE BOAT

MALTESE CROSS

HOLY STONE

SUEZ . CANAL .
COMPANIES . OFFICES

It was a grand send off and no mistake, and though I had been working on deck for nearly twentyfour hours, I forgot fatigue and was lost in wonder. When we got outside we found the Diana waiting for us, so we extinguished our illuminations, and turned our ships head for Port Said, the lights of the fleet being visable for some considerable time. The Andromeda remained behind to pickup mails, but she caught us up the following day, The next morning the sky became overcast, and remained so until the following evening when it began to rain. We run into Port Said, about half past four, passing a P&O liner and they cheered us as we passed; we made fast opposite the Pilot House and prepared for coaling; the Duke & Duchess made an official visit about 5.30. and inspected a company of the 2nd Scudenesse. returned to the ship soon after 6. p.m.. We started coaling about 10. pm, and it was like a babel to hear the incessant chanting and gibberish chatter of the natives, by 4 next morning all our coal was inboard, and by six we where under weigh and steaming slowly down the Seuz Canal, followed by a pilot Tug it was a very pleasant trip through the canal, but the weather was changing rapidly; getting hotter and hotter, now we would pass a caravan, and then a croud of Arab boys, who would run along the banks crying out for buiscuit, as far as the eye could reach on either side streat the sandy desert and when we

S.T. TITAN
ESCORTING US
THROUGH THE
SUEZ CANAL

came across a "Bringing to Station" with its few shrubs and palms the green was quite refreshing to the sight, At Ismalia we came across the Britannie and we found out that she carried a number of homeward troops, from Australia, and as we passed them they gave us three rousing cheers; which we returned with equal energy, our band then played Home sweet home & Auld lang syne, and it was peculiar how these familiar tunes touched our feelings, although we had only just left home. We dropped anchor in the evening in the Bitter lakes, and proceeded on our way first thing in the morning, passing two liners one a German; and one belonging to the same line as the Ophir. We arrived at Suez about 10 in the forenoon, and the Hussar a British gunboat saluted us, we anchored, but got up anchor again and proceeded on our way and at midday. We had a rather uneventfull voyage through the Red

GUARD SHIP   SUEZ

sea, except that we met the Cocatrice a British sloop and she signalled

H.M.S. HUSSAR.

a great capture of men stores and cattle by French. We passed through the Gates of Hell about midnight on friday, and arrived at Aden the following morn, where we met with our old acquaintances the Snr George & Juno, and the Snr George had one of the Royal steam boats out ready for use; as far as we could see from the ship.

Aden was entirely devoid of vegetation, nothing but rugged Vandyke brown coloured mountains surrounding the town, but the sea front and some parts of the town was very prettily decorated; their Royal Highnesses went ashore about 4 in the afternoon and returned about 7 in the evening. The Duke also gave orders for the Racoon gunboat to pay off; and she instantly hoisted the paying off pendan-

"HMS. COCATRICE"

In the evening the town illuminated as well as could be expected considering that they have only the primitive methods of light; The Egypt a stately liner also illuminated; so, did one or two other yatch's that lay in harbour; Whilst the Racoon had a design picked out in electric light; a crown under lined with a letter G and M representing the christian names of their Royal Highnesse's. A reception was given on board about nine for all the big nobs of the place including officers and wives of the troops stationed

H.M.S. Racoon at Aden

here; but every one was out of the ship by 11. pm and by half past we where under weigh, together with our escort. and bound for Colombo. Our trip to Colombo was not very eventfull except that a concert was given in the grand saloon and considering it was organ ised in very quick time; it was a

RED HAIRED NIGGER
ADEN

NATIVE BOAT ADEN

complete success, what had a lot to do with it wos we had a complete set of theatrical costumes, supplied by the court costumers, London. I give a programe of the events on the next page The weather now was very hot, and most men where in a

continual sweat from morn till night, during the day lots
of life was to be seen, shoals of flying fish, dolphin", ect could
he seen every where, some of them quite close. to the ship. We
arrived at Colombo early friday morning, and found it to
be a very beautifull place, with waving palms, and scyamore
more. stretching a way for miles; whilst
in the far distance was, a range of mountains
hardley visable. . The, town itself was
decorated every where, as well as all
the ships and boats in the harbour, prominent
amongst them being Liptons boats with a
great show of Irish ensigns flying. Their
Royal Highnesses went ashore at 1.pm
amidst the usual ceremony of salutes
after looking round Colombo, they proceeded

by train to Kandi, inspecting the native troops. and presenting
the Ceylon mounted infantry, with the Kings Colours and South African
war medals, the also witnessed some native dancing, snake charming
ect. The crew of the Ophir had a grand feed of fruit, pineapple,
bannana's, mangoes ect here, they where also invited to a feast
ashore but they did not go on account of coaling ship. The Planters
association also sent off several hundred pound cases of tea for
the ships crew, What amused me most here was the niggers
six or seven of them would come off to the ship on the trunk
a cocoanut tree; and standing up, would sing Ta-rara-boom-dea
making a smacking noise with the upper part of their arms against
the body, as an accompanyment, after which they would ask for
you to throw in money, for which they would dive like fish

seldom loseing the coin. The baats here are very curious being less than a foot in breadth, and kept from capsizing by means of an outrigger, or log of wood secured to two poles sticking out from the side of the baat, these baats are called Cattermerans

TA.RA.RA. BOOM. DE AY.

I went ashore Monday afternoon and found a great difference to any other place I had ever visited; 999 out of a thousand were blacks, and hardly one dressed the same, some with long hair some short, some with a pate shining like metal, in fact every design imagine able was used in dressing the hair, but the majority had it done up behind like a woman's, Nearly every one glided noiselessly about without shoes, and the beauty and richness of their appeareal surprised me, some of the better class wearing dresses together with jewelry, worth many thousands of pounds. In the evening, we, together with the three ship's of the East Indies squadron, and most of the merchant-men in harbour illuminated, and about half past 10, their Royal Highnesses and suite returned to the ship. About 8 in the morning the East Indies squadron together with our escort, went out of harbour and Admiral Bainbridge carried out steam tatics until half

COLOMBO
SCAVENGER
CROW

H.M.S. "HIGHFLYER."

H.M.S. "POMONE."

H.M.S. "MARATHON."

"East Indies Squadron"

past nine, when we slowly steamed round. The breakwater carefully picking our way amongst the swarms of native boats, and whilst the forts boomed out a Royal salute the St George and Juno took up their position in single line off our starboard quarter, and the Highflier and Pomone off the port quarter, and in this formation we proceeded on our way to Singapore. In the evening about 5 Oclock the whole of us hove to, and sent whatever mails we had to the Pomone, and when she had them all she left and being a very fast boat she was soon hull down. The Highflier meanwhile had steamed right round us and then came close up to us, her crew manned the rigging and they they gave us three hearty cheers, cheer such as only British seamen can give, we then gave three cheers for the Admiral, the Highflier then sheared off, the Juno then took up her position of the Port quarter and once more we proceeded on our way, nothing of interest taking place untill about 11 Oclock the first watch on Wednesday night when we caught a proper tropical shower

A Tropical Shower.

In these latitudes at this time of the year, it lightens incessantly, but to night the flashes where of extra brilliancy, showing in three or four places in the sky at once, not a breath of wind stirred the indigo waters and after a flash of lightening more vivid than any of the preceeding ones, a rumble of distant thunder shook the stillness, accompanied directley after by a rush off wind accompanied with extra large spots of rain, instantly the boson's mate roared, "close all ventalation", and then the fun began. A terrific crash of thunder broke overhead, and shook the ship throughout, and the lightening played with such dazzling brilliancy that our escort could be seen as plain as in broard daylight, although they where a mile away; and down came the rain, came down I say, I guess it was chucked down; it put me in mind as if the sea had been taken up to the clouds and then dropped in a lump; it was impossible to see now, the rain came with such force, in fact it was just the same as if a fire hose was being played full in the face, I believe the rain found its way into every part of the ship the Royal compartments suffering; but it was soon over, and a few minutes after the ship was quite dry, and in the distance the lightening played feebley. The following Saturday was kept as a Sunday, and early Sunday morn we ran into Singapore a very pretty, but, low lying, well wooded place, and went alongside the jetty and after their Royal Highnesses had departed commenced coaling at once, the coal was got in by Chinamen and they kept up a continual run all the day long, their peculiarity being to run when loaded and walk with empty baskets

CHINESE. COAL HEAVERS

We finished coaling about 5 in the evening and steamed round to the man of war anchorage, and anchored. Here we found, the Aurora. Arethusa Linnet. Rosario. Algerine.

belonging to the British China Squadron, also a Dutchman
a Frenchman and an Italian man of war. The following
morning a horde of Chinese painters came aboard and gave
us a complete coat of paint outside, which made us look

"H.M.S. RASARIO,"   " H.M.S. ALGERINE,"   " H.M.S. AURORA."

a little more respectable than we had been for some time, On
the next day a sad incident occured; a stoker who had been
ill some few days, suddenly died of disentry, and after consulting
the Commadore it was decided that he should be burried at sea
the same evening. To day was also a regetta for the natives

" FRENCH "   " DUTCH "   " ITALIAN "

and a verry pretty sight it was, expecrally the sailing
races with the crews dressed in every colour imagineable
There was also two or three Malay war canoes, which must
have been terrors in the earlier history of this place. They
raced round and round our ship time after time, keeping

"MALAY WAR CANOE"

up a continual din with their tom-toms, and every now and then giving vent to their feelings by an unearthly yell; a large number of natives came off in canoes; or at least logs of wood not much larger than themselves, hollowed out, and as fast as they filled with water they forced it out with a

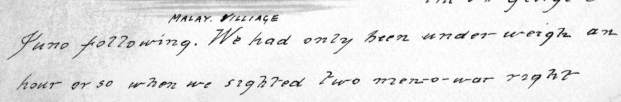

H.M.S. ARETHUSA.

peculiar motion of the feet, these men where far superior to those at Colombo, in diving for money. In the afternoon their Royal Highness came on board loaded with presents from the loyal natives, including a pair of Siameese kittens., named Rajar & Ranie. As soon as everything was on board. We got up anchor and admidst the thunder of the guns of all the men of war in the harbour we slowly steamed down the Sunda or at least the Mallacca Straits the St George & Juno following. We had only been under-weigh an hour or so when we sighted two men-o-war right

H,M,S, LINNET.

MALAY. VILLIAGE

ahead, which proved to be two Japanese battleships and as they drew alongside our starboard side they both saluted and the S.ᵗʰ George returned it. Just before

evening quarters
the fore topmen
had orders to lay
the port foremost
upper ladder flat
This was the first
thing towards the
funeral of our ship

JAPANESE. BATTLESHIP.S

mate who only died the same morning; the seamen act when only wearing duck trousers and flannels because of the heat of the tropics, but the bo-sons mate piped all men will attend divisions with their jumpers on; after divisions, the seamen and marines where marched on the promenade deck and fell in with with an open space reaching from forward aft. between them, and each man was served out with a prayer & hymn book; the little noise the men where making, was quickly hushed, when the strains of Chopins funeral march came softly from aft; Walking up the space between the men, came the stokers and mess mates of deceased; preceeded by the band Then came the Rev. Wood. followed by the corpse borne on the shoulders of six sturdy

FUNERAL AT SEA

stokers; as the mornful posession slowly passed up the avenue of soldiers, sailors, and marines; I noticed that several men where very much affected, The posession stopped and the corpse was placed on the upper part of the ladder already mentioned Over the body was placed a Union Jack, and on top was a beautiful wreath of white roses and maden-hair-fern. presented by Her Royal Highness The Duchess. The silence now was painfull but was relieved some-what when The Rev Wood began the funeral service and a loud splash followed the words commit his body to the deep; and as I glanced over the side all I could see was a shattered wreath floating on the the troubled waters A firing party of marines now fired three volleys over the spot, and then all hands joined in the hymn; A few more years shall roll, very softly at first but towards the end it gathered strength; and enabled most of those present to relieve their feelings in song; the Duchess and most of the ladies and gentlemen present seemed very much

affected right through the ceremony. expecially those that where roving the seas for the first time. About 9-30, the following evening a terrible voice, coming from over the bows, roared Ship—

CHINESE. JUNK.

Ahoy, a pause and then the same trumpet like voice continued, what ship is that, and wither bound, what cargo, ect. The officer on watch instantly replied, His

Britannic Majisties Yatch Ophir, bound for Australia, with
their Royal Highnesses, the Duke & Duchess of Cornwall & York
on board; the voice then answered, "As a messenger from old
King Neptune, I bid you welcome to his domains; and
he bids me to say that he will pay the ship a visit to morrow
with his wife and all his court," the officer on the bridge again
spoke, but no answer came back, no sound but the rush of water
from our bows, as we plowed our way across the Indian ocean
The next morning all was bustle and activity, all hands being
employed rigging up a huge bath in which father Neptune
was to baptise all the new entries entrusted to his care,
namely; all those that had never crossed the line before, The
navigator now said that we where rapidly nearing the line

CROSSING THE LINE

It was about ten O.Clock the following morn, when old Neptune
came aboard, making his appearence in a chariot composed
of huge sea shells, the raw jagged edges edged with rope
that had the appearence of belonging to some ship of a
bygone age. Upon reaching the promenade deck, three representative
one of Britannia one Australia and one Canada, stepped
into the chariot and then the whole lot glided for-ward
drawn by the Guard of honour; composed of the biggest marines
in the ship, and dressed in all the outlandish costumes possible

I noticed that all the ladies and gentlemen belonging to
the Royal suite, where very busy with their cameras.
When Neptune accompanied by his wife and the whole of
his court reached the fore end of the deck, close to the
large tank; he was received by their Royal Highnesses
the Duke and Duchess; after a few words of greeting.
Neptune stepped from his charriot and carrying
A silver goblet in his hand, walked up to the Duchess
and sprinkled water on her head, saying at the same time
It makes me feel most happy, in the name of Salt water,
to christen you Queen of the Seas; Ampitrite then stepped
forward and presented the Duchess with a bouquet of coral

NEPTUNE'S GOBLET.

of great beauty; Neptune meanwhile
christening the remainder of the ladies
as soon as he finished he decended to a
large platform over looking the tank
accompanied by his secatary, barbers
and the remainder of his court; and then
the ball opened. His secetary unrolled a large parchment
and readd out the roll of Greenhorns and Goshens, beginning
with the Duke himself; the Duke instantly stepped
forward, and seated himself in the chair placed at
the very edge of the platform over looking the canvas
tank, and was instantly seized by Neptunes barbers
and duly lathered and scraped in the orthodox stile,
and then pitched head over heels into the tank, where
he recieved his babtism at the hands of the sea bears

in the tank, who gave him a severe ducking, admidst the laughter of the Duchess, and suite, and the whole of the assembled ships company; but no time could be lost, and the Secetary instantly called out the next one to be babtised

NEPTUNE, HIS WIFE, AND CHILDREN.

and then the next, and so on, each officer and man suffering according to his popularity, some where litterally lathered from head to foot with the vile compound Old Neptune's barbers used

COMING EVENT CAST THEIR SHADOWS BEFORE

and then nearly drowned in the tank; and woe be to the man that attempted to remonstrate; if he opened his mouth it was instantly filled up with lather from a large syringe deftly used by Neptunes

physician and if violent was soon passified by the Guard
of honour, one of them being the Champion heavy weight
lifter of the Navy and Army. The fun was now at its
height, and to increase it a stiff breeze sprang up from
South-west, bringing with it an heavy swell, which made
the water in the tank like unto a tempestuous sea, and washed
babtised and babtisers about like corks; towards the
end of the ceremony one of the men whilst being flung into
the tank, managed to bring one of the barbers with him
And another whose feelings where hurt by rough usage made
a desperate charge and shoved the heavy weight-lifter
in on top of him, then dozens of bluejackets joined in
the general melee, when all of a sudden one side of the
tank collapsed and washed the whole lot down the
waterways, and when they where gathered up;
Neptune, Ampitrite and the whole of his court had
dissapeared, gone, but not forgotten, To day was the 25th of
April, and already the weather was rapidly getting colder
and the sea, and sky, resuming that leaden colour so often
seen round the coast of England, on the 29th we ran away

ALBATROSS

from our escort and the
following night we ran
into Albany in the
province of Western
Australia; and

landed, Sir Arthur Lawley, the govenor of this province; as
he left the ship; the ships company gave three hearty cheers

We left early the following morning, as we passed out by one entrance, we perceived our old friends the "S.t George and Juno" creeping in by another; It was now quite as cold as when we left England, and large numbers of those gigantic sea birds called Albatross's followed day and night in our wake, it was most bewitching to watch these mighty birds; for hours they would keep up with the ship without a motion of the wings, skimming along as if secured to the ship by a line, now and then with the tips of their huge wings dipped an inch or so in the water. On the 5.th of May we dropped anchor off Snapper Point, about 30 or 40.mls from Melbourne; here Lord Hopetown paid us a visit, and dined with their Royal Highnesses. As we approached this place, we where met by four ships of the Australian Squadron, the Royal Arthur flagship, and the Ringarooma, Wallaroo, Mildura, and also our old chum

PART OF THE
AUSTRALIAN
SQUADRON

ROYAL ARTHUR
RINGAROOMA
WALLAROO
MILDURA

the Juno, followed an hour or so afterwards by the S.t George, they all dropped anchor with us here; the next morning we all proceeded on our way to Melbourne, the Ophir leading; About half 10 in the fore noon we sighted a gigantic Russian warship off our starboard bow, looking bigger still in the morning mist, which the sun had not yet dispersed, next we sighted a Yankee Cruiser, then a

Netherlands cruiser, and finally two German cruisers
Just before we dropped anchor; the whole of the warships
both British and Foreign opened fire in a Royal salute;
and as the Sun was now rapidly clearing away the mist,
a brilliant scene presented itself to our view. We dropped

anchor about midday, and were soon.

surrounded by pleasure steamers, or

hurrah boats as they called on account

of the amount of cheering their

passengers indulge in,

and the sun shone out

brilliantly welcome

ing us to the fair

land of

Australia

Our Stay in Australia

MELBOURNE

Their Royal Highnesses went ashore about 2 in the afternoon
in a beautifull paddle steamer. the "Hygeia," accompanied
by the whole of their suite, and met with a splendid
reception at the St Kilda pier. Under the cloudless sky
the St Kilda pier was a very pretty sight. It's great length
was emphasised by a crimson carpet, running along the centre
from end to end, and rows of masts, from which flew brightly

colored pennants, the shelter shed was made quite beautiful.
Midway was a handsome arch, erected by the St Kilda yatch
men, and at the place, of landing, a canopy which was festuned
and draped, Never before was the pier such a centre of attraction. The Esplanade and its stands were thronged with
people, and every window commanding a view of the scene was
occupied, Then on the bay side, was the Royal Yacht "Ophir,"

St KILDA and PRAHRAN ARCH

and all the British and Foreign men of war, with a background
of white smoke, the remnant of the Royal salute they had
thundered out during the passage of the Royal party from
ship to shore. The pier was lined on both sides by the Vic
torian Permanent Artillery, and the 1st battalion Infantry
Brigade. It was just 5 minutes to 2 when the Royal visitors
walked down the gangway from the "Hygeia," and were
received by His Excellency the Governon-General. This was
the signal for loud and continued cheers of welcome
from the immence crouds of enthusastic Britishers
                                                    & Colonials

I will now leave their Royal Highnesses, as every one must
be familliar with the enthusiastic reception the loyal
Australians gave to the eldest son and daughter in law
of our most noble King. I will now try and describe the way
in which Melbourne was decorated in honour of the great
event. In the first place Melbourne is a fine city in itself

CHINEE ARCH   DUKE'S ARCH

and add to it decorations far surpassing anything we have
ever attempted in England it presented a magnificent sight.
Triumphial arches that presented as good a spectical by
day as by night, illuminated fountains, all the principal
houses and shops were illuminated from chimney to door-step.
Mirriads of banners flags and streamers, and last but not
least a teeming population of "Britishers" to the backbone,
who where every ready to pass a cheering remark, or give a
harty slap on the back of any jolly tar they passed, especially
if he belonged to the "Ophir". In the afternoon after the
Duke and Duchess had landed we placed the Ophir along

side one of the piers, and we where shortly followed by the S.t George
and Juno; and then the Australian ships followed suit. The next day
we started to coal and about midday the hugh. Russian cruiser and
the American cruiser took up their positions alongside one of the piers next
to us. Port watch went on sixty hours leave the next day and came
back with wonderfull stories of how good the people had been to them

RUSSIAN, CRUISER, GROMOBOI   U.S.S. BROOKLYN

On friday evening my own watch (starboard) went on their
sixty hours leave, Of course the city itself lay about 3 miles

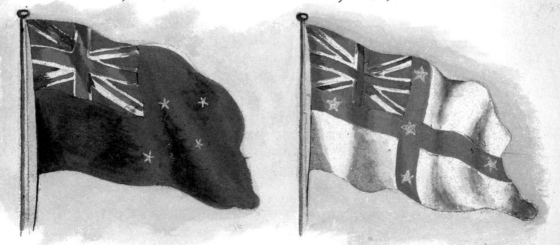

POPULAR AUSTRALIAN FLAGS

from the seafront and we went up by train, and I soon noticed
that the carriages where much better fitted up than those
in the old country. When we arrived at Melbourne we where

surprised to hear that we where to travel free of charge. As
I walked out of the station, I was at once filled with
amazement at the beauty of the scene which presented
itself to my astonished gaze, each side of the wide streets

GERMAN. CRUISER. HANSA.

as far as the eye could reach, was one mass of coloured
bunting and silk; tall and gaily festuned venetian
masts. running from end to end, interupted only by a
triumphal arch here and there. Each arch had a name
the Chinese arch was built by the Chinese, and was very
picturesque; A most novel arch was the one built entirely
of boxes of butter, representing the daily amount of
butter exported from this place; the design being
a Norman gateway; The Queen arch was of very
original design, but I dont think it proved the success
the designer thought it would. The King arch was

grand, and very much admired, the Dukes arch was very
much on the same scale and colouring. The city and the
citizens arch where magnificent structures of ancient
Roman design; in fact they where all very good and it is
impossible for me to put all I saw and heard into this

BUTTER ARCH   KINGS. ARCH.

book, but all this show was nothing compared with the people
they where grand and no mistake, even without an exception
and its true when I say that I was treated better than if

GERMAN. CORVETT   H. M COLONIAL. SHIP CEREBOS   DUTCH CRUISER

I was at home with relations and friends, it did not matter
which way one turned, you met with a cheering remark though
I must say that the "Ophir's" came in for the greatest share
of the good feeling the people displayed. and I assure you

it was with a feeling of deep regret that I returned to the ship. On the afternoon that I returned to the ship it was open to visitors and I shall never forget the immense crowds that continually came and went, it was a regular crush on board but the best of good feeling prevailed, the bluejackets doing everything they could for their guests as I may call them, and as the evening drew on a space we had our work cut out to get the ship, cleared thousands of them remained on the pier alongside the ship. At eight o.clock exact, every man-of-war burst forth into light, and although I have seen a lot of naval illuminations I can safely say that these where the best I had ever seen, and gentle reader dont be offended when I say that the Foreign men-of-war beat us hollow in the way they dressed their ships; but bear in mind that they must have spent a great deal of time and trouble in getting ready, whilst our ships where at drill, and getting ready for something more serious than illuminating ship. But the British boys in blue where not to be done and nearly all our ships companies made up an extempor concert on the upper deck; which amused the crowds on the jetty immensely. The following morning we heard that our programe was to be altered; Their Royal Highnesses where going to Brisbane by train, as there was a slight attack of plague at the place, and if they made their visit by the sea the "Ophir" would have to go into quarantine for perhaps a fortnight; which would have altogether upset more important engagements. So on saturday the 18th of May, about midday it was with a heavy heart that we cast off from the pier; amidst the cheers, waving of handkerchiefs, ect of the many kind friends we had made in the fair city of "Melbourne", and steamed

H.M.S. St. GEORGE.

out past the foreign men-of-war on our way to "Sidney", Our escort comprising the St. George only. We arrived at "Sidney" on Monday morning and were at once struck with the magnificence of the harbour, As yet very little had been done in the manner of decoration; the following morning we went in dock, and had our bottom scraped and painted; came out again the following

day and went alongside the coaling warf at garden island,
and took in a very large quantity of coal: On friday we left
for the Hawksbury river, to embark their Royal Highnesses.
arriving there the middle of the day, this river has been
most appropreately named the "Australian Rhine", as its
beauties are of the best and rarest.. The next day their
Royal Highnesses arrived by the stern weel steamer the
Captain Cook; or at least the General Gardon, I should say,
and escorted by the Captain Cook, Their Royal Highnesses did not
look much the worse for their prolonged stay on shore The
next day the Royal party had a delightful picnic up the river

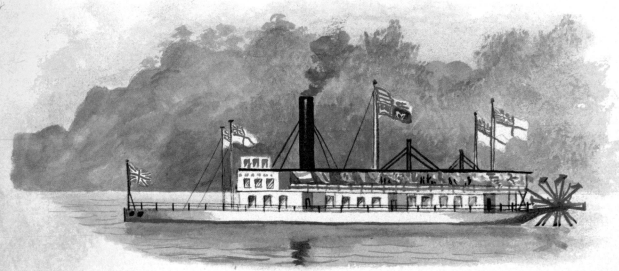

STERN WHEEL, STEAMER GENERAL GORDON.

in the "General Gordon," when they returned I noticed that
the captain of the boat was in the seventh heaven of delight
at the honour, I suppose of taking the Duke and Duchess for the
trip, and he left us an happy man, with a present from the Duke
I dont know what it was; to day was the Duchess's birthday
and the ships dressed rainbow fashion and fired a salute

In the evening the Duchess sent word to the men that they could drink her health on her birthday; rum was served out on the upper deck, and both the Duke and Duchess had a tot of Navy Rum too, The Duke then stepped foreward and said he had been asked by the Duchess to thank the ships company for their kind wishes for her birthday; The whole ships company then gave three ringing cheers, and the band played god bless the "Prince of Wales." A most laughable incident now occured, one man started to sing; She's a jolly good fellow, and the whole ships company took it up and gave it lip, the Duchess seemed greatly amused, the men then gave three more cheers, and then spliced the main brace in true nautical style I may here mention that this was the second time we spliced the main brace, the first time being at the Dukes invitation the day we crossed the line, The next day we got up anchor, and made for "Sydney", As soon as we got outside, we where met by the Australian fleet, who saluted us and then took up their positions astern of our escort the S⁺ George & Juno.

Sydney

THE HEADS

The sun shone forth brilliantly as we passed between the

Heads. The most prominent points where thronged with people and there was plenty of waving handkerchiefs, but very little cheering, as we slowly made our way up the beautiful harbour of Sydney; Numbers of pleasure steamers of a distint yankee pattern, and thronged with people, came and met us; As we got closer to the town, we found another portion of the Australian squadron there, and also the huge Russian Cruiser from "Melbourne," who at once saluted us, together with the shore batteries; it was in the midst of all this din that we made fast to a buoy in "Farm Cove," opposite "Government House" and close to a small island which used to be of great use for the safe keeping of prisoners in the days of transportation. It was about 2-p-m when their Royal Highnesses went ashore; dence crowds of spectators surrounded the landing place, The

ROYAL PULLING BARGE

Royal pulling barge conveyed their Royal Highnesses from the Ophir to the shore, where they met with a hearty reception, and then drove to Government House by a roundabout rout so, as to view the decorations. Starboard

watch, my own, went on sixty hours leave in the evening, and
when I went ashore, I met with a great dissappoint, I expected
to find Sydney like Melbourne, but there was no comparison;
not only where the streets narrow and badley paved; but
the decorations where very meagre; in fact it was an
insult to call them decorations at all; after Melbourne;
there was only two arches and these nothing to the ones at
Melbourne, But I believe the reason was that they had their

ENTRANCE TO GOVERNMENT. HOUSE

day when they celebrated the Inauguration of the Commonwealth
the people also where very different and seemed more distant
and stuck up, in fact the only place that not only I, but,
all my chums took a fancy to, was the "Royal. Naval. House,"
The Duke himself paid a visit to this place, and was so
pleased with it, that he personly complimented J. Shearston
the owner, and presented a large signed photo of himself

and the Duchess to the house; The people of Sydney seemed greatly impressed by the Russian Cruiser, and reckoned that she was a match for the remainder of the ships in the harbour, britishers included, put together. One evening was devoted by the ships of war, to illuminating, and as at "Melbourne," the foreigners knocked us out of time, but towards the later part of the evening, the Australian ships took the cake by making a water fall of fireworks, fall from their upper decks into the water, and it made a magnificent

H.M.S "BOOMERANG"   "H.M.S. KARAKATTA"

sight, and was prolonged for nearly an hour. The last two or three days of our stay, visitors where allowed on board and the Duke went shooting up country, It was on the morning of the 6th of June when their Royal Highnesses embarked and by twelve midday, we where slowly steaming down the harbour, with our escort in our wake bound for "New Zealand," The shores where much more crowded than when we came in ten days before.

New Zealand.

MAORI IDOL

Auckland

We arrived at Devonport; a place quite close to "Auckland" on the 10th. Here we witnessed quite a unique incident; i.e. we perceived a small boat making for the ship, and as it got closer, we saw that a little girl was the sole occupant, she was a white girl, and no older than 10 yrs at the outside; she pulled beautifully, and came up along side in grand stile, although a nasty sea was running, One of the side boys went down the gangway to meet her, and she gave him a beautifull bouquet, and asked him to give it to the Duchess, needless to say it was accepted

The following morning the got up anchor and proceeded to Auckland, Over a dozen large passenger boats came out to meet us; and took up there positions astern, As we drew closer to our destination, we saw the shore was crowded with people, and they cheered themselves hourse, as we came up alongside the jetty. Their "Royal Highnesses" went ashore about 2 in the afternoon and met with a

AUCKLAND HARBOUR BOARD ARCH

great reception. An electric button was fitted up on the jetty so that "His Royal Highness" announced to the whole of Auckland his own landing. A splendid triumphal arch made of greenstuff, was erected at the head of the pier, and another at the other end representing two lighthouses. joined by an arched span. Dense masses of people lined the route right to "Government House," and cheered again and again as their "Royal Highnesses," and escort, drove by. During our stay in Auckland the "Duke & Duchess" witnessed some Native dancing

or as the Maori's call it Haka, it is a kind of war
dance, and without a doubt is the best style of savage
dancing that one would find, if he searched the whole
World over, To show what kind
of people the "Maories" are, I
relate the following; It appears
that the evening before the
Duke's visit, a great calamity
fell on the natives, one of
there greatest chiefs died
Now this race bewails; loud
and long; for day's; at the death of any notable chief;

TAMATI WAKA NENE
A FAMOUS N.Z. CHIEF

but; this time, no one outside
their own circle knew any
thing about it, untill the
Duke came and went, and
then, and not till then, did
the sounds of sorrow rise up
into the air; The Duke also

KYWI

had some very good shooting, and bagged about 2 stags
and 6 hinds. "New Zealand" has some peculiar birds, and
I give an illustration of the most peculiar. It was late
in the evening of the 15th when their Royal Highnesses
went ashore, and at daybreak the next morning we
let go our hawsers, and turned our ships head for

Wellington, N.Z. When we got fairly out to sea, we found a heavy ground swell running, which made us pitch and roll a good deal; one of our escorts the Juno, took a different course to us, and we soon lost sight of her; the next day was spent at sea, and the weather was getting very miserable

HARBOUR BOARD ARCH

very cold, and a drizzling rain falling most of the time; in the evening we ran into "Wellington" harbour, it was about 7 p.m. and a dinner party was held on board, and the Govenor and others of note came off to the ship, We also found the same portion of the Australian squadron here that was at "Melbourne" Our trip from Auckland to Wellington was done in very good time nearly 600 miles in less than 48 hours

Wellington. N.Z.

The sort of weather we got at
Wellington

On the morning of the 18ᵗʰ June, admidst the thunder
of saluting guns; we made our way carefully along
side the jetty of "Breezy Wellington" as it is called
The weather was shocking, but cleared up a bit by
the time their Royal Highnesses landed, which
they did about 11 a.m; and as they drove through
the dock gates, they met with a most enthuastic
reception, and to make things better the sun made
several attempts to break through the heavy low
lying clouds, and made things livelier, Taking the
weather into consideration, their "Royal Highnesses"

had a remarkable drive through the city; the people thronged every available place along the whole line of route to Government House. The place to was most exceeding, well decorated, there being quite as many triumphal arches as there was at Melbourne, and one of them the (coal arch) beating all other arches we had yet seen. Altogether, taking into considering the sise of the place, there was an extraordinary show of

Bluejacket coaling ship

patriotic feeling. The day before leaving, a regetta was held in which the Navy played a prominent part One thing I wish to mention is that this was the first place where the crew of the Ophir coaled ship, and we took in 800 tons, the above illustration shows the manner

which the bluejackets and marines, carried the coal, and you
will understand it was exceedingly hard work when I say that each
basket was about two cwt. During the regetta 3 submarine
mines as they are commonly called where exploded one after
the other, each blowing to atoms small representations of ships
placed directly over   each mine.

NAVAL
SUBMARINE
MINE

SUBMARINE EXPLOSION

On Friday June the 21st about half past 3 in the afternoon Their "Royal Highnesses" embarked, and immediatly
we cast of from the jetty; and despite the wretched weather
the shore was crowded with people, who cheered again
and again, as we swung our ships head for the mouth
of the harbour; and together with our escort proceeded

on our way to "Lyttelton" Two or three pleasure steamers
accompanied us out of the harbour, but they soon found
the sea to rough, and our speed to fast, and they turned
back, It was quite dark by the time we got out to sea.
The sea was pretty rough, and all along the coast
at intervals huge beacons had been lit, and fairly
lit up the coast line; we where of "Lyttelton" very
early next morning, and as soon as it was daylight
proceeded up the harbour, passing five ships of the
Australian squadron who manned yards and
saluted us, their ships companies cheering meantime
We tied up alongside of a jetty, with a landing
place all ready rigged up. with green stuff, and
bunting. The Duke and Duchess and suite left the
ship about 11 in the forenoon, and just before they
stepped into the train that was to convey them
to Christchurch, a large body of school children
sang ("God Save the King") in good time, and good
voice; the Duke and suite saluting meanwhile; They
then stepped into the train admidst the cheers of
the crowd, And then the train steamed slowly
on its way to the beautifull city of "Christchurch"
The train had to pass through an exceedingly long
tunnel, as Lyttelton is completely surrounded by mountains.

Lyttelton Canterbury and Christchurch

The weather here was bright and clear but very cold; and the train service free to the men of the visiting warships, so I made use of the opportunity and made a flying visit to "Christchurch," and

H.M.S. PYLADES   H.M.S. ARCHER   H.M.S. SPARROW   H.M.S. TORCH

found it a flourishing town, the decorations to were on a very lavish scale, and the arches very original, one being built of ice and frozen meat, and bearing the inscription (Frozen our product but warm our welcome) and another formed of livestock in cages including, cows, horses, sheep, poultry, ect. The town also, was well illuminated as darkness set in.

The next day instead of going by train I climbed the high hills that lay between us and Christchurch and when I reached the top a glorious panarama presented itself to my gaze, a flat plain that at first looked like the sea, lay at my feet, but as I gazed I could just make out the tops of the

CHRISTCHURCH FROM THE HILLS

steeples and tall chimneys peeping through the mist; whilst away in the far distance, was a range of noble mountains, It was a splendid sight and well worth the hard walk over the boulder strewn hills. I also visited a Maori village. but met with a dissapointment, I expected to find them in a semi civilised condition, but judge to my surprise when I found them exactly the same as the Europeans Same houses, same dress, same speach, in fact yust the same as English people, but for their brown skins, The sketch below was taken up the river, some fifteen miles above Christ church where as you can see, the scenery was most

·Sunrise in New Zealand·

bewitching, but a hard frost setting in, as soon as the sun went down made matters a little bit disagreeable, to us, who only a short time ago, where under a scorching tropical sun

About midday on the 27th of June we slipped from the warf and went outside, returning again in the evening, after having adjusted our compasses, and dropped our anchor in the gulf some distance from "Lyttelton," A heavy swell was running and made us roll considerably. It was about 8 pm, when we perceived the "Goveners yacht approaching with the Royal Party on the saloon deck, she was brilliantly lit up with electricity, and as she came on rockets ascended in all directions. When she came closer we saw that there would be some difficulty in getting their "Royal Highnesses" from one ship to the other, the swell was so great, but after considerable trouble a gangboard was got out, and wating their first opportunity the Royal Party quickly ran on board the Duchess first, the Duke following; and only just in time; for the two ships came together with a crash and then rolled far apart, leaving the gangboard dangling down from the Ophir's upper deck, One of our principal gangway ladders was smashed to matchwood also the lower boom, a long spar some fifteen or sixteen inches in diameter, A lot more damage was done but the Governers yacht suffered the most, she having some of her plates stove in and her bridge smashed, and after we got the "Royal Suite" and luggage on board, she left with all possible speed for "Lyttelton" to go in dock, and we got up anchor and proceeded on our way for "Tasmania"; our escort

Wardroom & Crew

PROVISIONING SHIP

"THE CREW'S SHARE"

THE WARDROOM'S SHARE

taking up their usual positions astern. The next morning was beautiful and clear, and the view shoreward was magnificent, the bright blue sea, and the light green hills, backed by hills of somber brown, behind which, towering into the purple sky was a range of noble snow capped mountains, making a grand picture. After passing through "Cooks Straits" we had a fair wind, and as we got further away from land the sea began to get rougher, and by midnight, the following day our good ship was rolling and tumbling about as bad, if not worse, than when we crossed the Bay, we shipped plenty of water and every place had a good share of it, I think the bakehouse suffered the most; I looked in and found the poor baker up to his waist in water loaves of bread, buns, dough, bags of flour, dishes baking tins ect. Several men where injured, and the Duchess must have been very ill; for as I have already mentioned, she was a victim to Mal-de-mere. Most of the suite did not venture out of their cabins, but the "Duke" seemed quite at home;

a regular Sailor Prince, The ships company especially
the seamen; where highly delighted with the turn
of events; as to day was "Sunday", and they knew that
there would be no divisions; a thing most + flat-foots
dread; as a most minute inspection is carried out
then, On the mess deck they amused themselves by

GALE BETWEEN. N.Z. & TASMANIA

yelling like fiends; every time a sea came down the
hatchway, and as this point of our journey was really
the begining of our homeward passage. they sang their
old favourite song (Rolling home to Merry England)
again and again, with great emphasis, The next day,
the wind moderated a little; and the sea was much smoother
We arrived at Hobart about 11 a.m. the 2nd of July.

+ Naval slang for "seaman.

Hobart
Tasmania

The following day we went alongside the pier, and I may state that they had prepared a much better landing stage, than we had previously met with in our tour. The people seemed exceedingly loyal, and the crisp bright wintry day, echoed and reechoed with hearty cheers; when their "Royal Highnesses" landed shortly after midday, The decorations also were very good, ferns like those in the illustration being largely used in the place of venetian masts, to line the streets, One of the principal events was the

wood chopping contest, The champion wood chopper being
present, I was not present myself but I heard Their Royal
Highnesses were greatly impressed by the way huge trees were
felled and cut up, in an increditably short space of time
What took my eye was "Mount Wellington" that formed the
background of "Hobart," and as a lot of my shipmates said
it would take a lot of climbing; In fact some said it would
take a day to get up, I said I would go to the top plant
a flag and be down the same day starting when we went
ashore

The ascent of Mount Wellington.

I started about 1 p.m. and after buying a cheap flag
which I meant to fix on the highest point, (The flag by the
way was a French flag the only one available all the others
having been sold) It was a walk of about six miles; to the
foot of the mountain, I may here mention that a road
led about two thirds of the way up, but as I never asked
for information, I was ignorant of the fact until afterwards
But any how I struck a timber track and started upwards
in good sprits, but bad boots, These boots where the cause

of much misery and hardship; in fact they where only a kind of leather slipper, served out to the seamen of the "Ophir," so as not to make a noise, when running about the ship, on the days we where supposed to wear boots, Sundays. ect And the sailors gave them the glorified name of the "Royal Pumps." Well after following the timber track for about a mile; passing many fallen monarchs of the forrest, it ended in a couple of small paths, hardly traceable in places, I followed the one I thought best and soon found myself in the thick of the forrest. The scenery was grand, nearly all the trees, were stripped of their bark, and stood up like columns of light against the dark background, on some of the trees the bark hung in long festunes from the branches

IN THE FOREST.

a hundred feet from the ground, and the gentle breeze swung it backward's and forward, like an immense pendulum., making a peculiar rattling sound, as it touched the neighbouring tree trunks. The under groath now began to get so thick it was well nigh impassable, and I noticed that a large number of the fallen trees had been brought down by fire; but no trace of fire could be seen in the underwood. It was astonishing how the fire had hardened the burnt trees. In some places the remnants of a tree stood up several feet burnt out to a fine point as hard and sharp as a needle. The ground began to change, it rar up much steeper, the trees smaller, and in place of the tangled underwood; were rocks; all sizes, intermingled with a long dry tough grass, that came in very handy in hanling ones self from rock to rock, I now paused to take a breath, and look round. I could not see the top of the mountain, it was enveloped in clouds, but I had a splendid view of the town, the harbour, and the shipping. But I had no time to loose if I was going to reach the summit, which I had told my shipmates I intended doing. So I once more started upwards, it was now about 5 p.m. as near as I could guess, as I had no watch, and felt like sitting down to a good tea, I now began to find snow in between the rocks, and I began to get so thirsty that from time I quenched it with pieces of frozen snow, The rocks now got bigger and bigger, and the side of the mountain steeper, and now and then the clouds would drift by and expose the mountain top to view, but it seemed a long way off yet; but I still struggled on the snow getting deeper the crust of which was frozen hard, and would bear ones weight—

IN. THE SNOW LINE

but now and then it would give way and I found myself in different depths up to ten or twelve feet. but I managed to extract myself each time from these awkward positions. My feet now began to get in a shocking state, the snow turned my "Royal pumps" into raw hide again, and made it a very slippery job climbing from rock to rock. The patches of snow where now 20 or 30 ft in extent, and I crossed these on my hands and knees, not knowing to what depth I may desend, if the hard crust gave way, I now came to a wall of rock sixty feet high, and as I saw no other way of getting up proceeded to climb it inch by inch. foot by foot until I reached the top. Snow was now falling in sheets, winding about in all directions, and I waited till it lifted a little, when I saw what appeared to be the summit a few hundred feet in front and above me. I now began to feel the cold, but I pushed on as it was rapidly getting dark, and passing an half dead tree broke off a branch about 15 feet in length. to act

HAULING UP
THE FLAG
STAFF

as a flag staff. When I reached what I thought was the top the view was rather clear, and I perceived the rocks ran up much higher yet, but I struggled on determined not to give in, After climbing another pile of rocks, I was enveloped in another snow cloud, as cold as ice; and the wind blew half a gale, the snow drifting by in heaps, all was black now except the snow; I found shelter between

THE SUMMIT

two large rocks, and waited for it to blow over I felt like lying down and going to sleep, but having read in books, it's fatal to do so in such cases, fought hard against the feeling. But the snow blast went as quickly as it came, and the moon shone out cold and clear. So I clambered on the largest rock and saw to my great joy that at last I was on the top, at last I had arrived at the topmost peak; so I quickly bound flag to the branch, and jammed it down between two rocks. It was as much as I could do, the cold was so intense, so I started to desend as quickly as possible, but not the same way as I came up, I soon came to a bit of a gully, the snow sloping away into the darkness beneath, I meant to cross this, but in doing so, started to slide downwards, so I turned on my back, and dug my heels deep into the snow, this checked me, but then the idea struck me, to slide down the mountain side, I was getting desperate, and would do anything to get out of the icy atmosphere. So away I slid into the darkness. I was thankfull afterwards that I did not go over a precipice; but I did not care at the time, for was I not getting to warmer air, away from the rocks, frost, and snow. I think I must have desended, several hundred feet like this when I found the bushes and rocks getting too thick to tobaggan any farther; so I started to clamber over the rocks once more; letting myself down by the grass and bushes. The moon was now shining brightly and after toiling for an hour or more, over rougher ground than any previously met with; I began to feel warmer; the thick bush, and tangled masses of vegetation again putting in an appearance, and the farther I desended into the forrest the darker it became; untill I could not see an arm's length in front of me; for the trees were so high that the moon failed to penetrate; and so I toiled on through the thick bushes, barking my shins against fallen timber falling over tree trunks, with only one, or at least a part of one shoe on, the other having dissapeared long ago; now and then a branch knocked my cap off, and I had difficulty in finding it again even with the aid of matches, which I luckily possessed, as I desended the ground got moister and in some places I went in up to my knees, a kind of stinging nettle also gave me a lot of inconvenience, and from time to time a thorn entered my feet, even penetrating the odd shoe; and I thought what a fool I was to venture on such a trip alone and at such a time, But I had the consolation that I had accomplished my task, and it was close on midnight when I stumbled across a road, yes a regular smooth flat road, and I was as happy as a king, After walking some distance, I came to an hotel, and as they had not retired I was able to get refreshments; and they seemed immencly surprised when I said I had just come from the mountain top and all alone, I left there about half past twelve and after walking another six miles, arrived on board more dead than alive, The next morning with the aid of a powerfull glass the flag could be seen from the ship, but I had to go to bed with bad feet and aching limbs

THE CONSEQUENCES

I dont know much about the next few days, that is of the outside world as I was hors-de-combat. but their "Royal Highnesses" had a good send when we left on the sixth; by the amount of noise and cheering outside. The next time I came on deck, I found we where anchored off the mouth of the river leading up to "Port Adelaide, Their "Royal Highnesses" left the ship the following day, and next morning we went up the river, and tied up alongside jetty.

Adelaide.
South Australia.

Going up the river to Adelaide greatly resembles the Suez Canal; the river being very narrow, and the land lying very low, stretching away for miles. A very pretty landing stage was erected. on the jetty, made of evergreens and sheaves of corn and wheat relieved, with coats of

arms etc, I believe their "Royal Highnesses"
had a grand time ashore; I am sure the "Ophir's"
ships company did. Our band gave three concerts
in the "Town Hall," which were well attended
Our theatrical troup also gave a concert
which was much appreciated; although the attend
ance was not great; owing to greater counter
attractions. The following friday was visitors
day, and I can safely say we had more people
on board. than we have, had, on any previous
occasion; It is quite enough; when I say that
quite a number of ladies fainted, and the
bluejackets and marines had their hands full.
But I think the principal feature of their
"Royal Highnesses" stay in Adelaide, was the
most enthusiastic send off they had when leaving
It was early in the morning of the 15th of July;

when the people began to assemble round and
about the jetty where the "Ophir" lay; by mid
day dense masses of people had arrived; and
with them came about 300 little boys and girls
dressed in sailors clothes, the boys carrying a small
wooden cutlass, and the girls
"small "Union Jacks," a "Guard
of Honour" was also drawn
up on the platform leading
from the train to the ship.
About one o'clock the train

One of the
Ophirs pets a
Laughing Jackass

H.M. Colonial. Ship. "Protector."

conveying their "Royal Highnesses" arrived and
was heralded by the cheers of the multitude;
As soon as the "Royal Party" had alighted; and
shaken hands, and wished good bye to their large
number of friends; they proceeded on board, The
"Duke" hardly looking so well as usual; but the
Duchess looked radiant with heath and beauty.
The suite also looked in good health and sprits
About 2 p.m we proceeded to cast off from the
Jetty and a couple of tugs hauled us off, As soon
as we began to move; the cheers were deffening
and above all could be heard the boys and girls
before mentioned; They even stood on their toes
in giving full force to their lungs, With their
wooden swords and flags waving frantically
in the air, Our band now began to play "Auld

Lang—Syne", and a hush fell on the crowd;
the "Royal Party" on the promenade deck drinking
their health meanwhile; I saw several women and
men with tears in their eyes as the old familiar
tune was heard; one old lady was crying out right,
and many a heart must have gone thousands of
miles across the sea; to the dear old "Home Land".
The instant the band finished, a cheer went up
simultainiously, and must have been heard for miles.
The band now played "Rule Britannia" and we proceed
ed down the river; escorted by H.M.C.S, Protector.
When we got to the mouth of the river; we found
the Royal Arthur awaiting to escort us to
                    Freemantle

In the
great Australian
Bight
—
Sunset

H.M.S. "Royal Arthur."

Our passage across the great "Australian Bight" was rather stormy, and gradually increased in vlence; in the next few days, especially; when

Wild life in
Australia
The Cassowary

we altered course, and turned up the west coast. On the friday we where close to "Freemantle"

THE "S.S. BRITANNIC" WITH AUSTRALIAN TROOPS HOMEWARD BOUND FROM "SOUTH AFRICA," ENTERING ALBANY.

but the weather was now so bad that it was thought adviseable to turn back, and run into Albany; which we did and arrived there about 2-a.m. on Sunday; and about 7-a.m. went right up the harbour, and made fast to the railway jetty! Our arrival causing no small stir amongst the few people left in the town; as most of them had gone up to "Freemantle" by train. In the afternoon we sighted a large white steamer off the mouth of the harbour, which turned out to be the "SS Britannic" with "Australian Bushmen" homeward bound from "S.Africa". This was the seccond time we met with this beautiful ship carrying troops. When we perceived that she was coming up the harbour; we turned up the band and all hands, as also did the "Royal Arthur." I forgot to mention that our two watchdogs where

here the "St George and Juno", Well as the "Britannic" passed between us and the "Royal Arthur", our crew gave three rousing cheers; repeated on the "Britannic" by the Bushmen, who went nearly mad when they recognised the "Duke and Duchess", The "Arthurs" now began to cheer, followed by the "Juno's" and our band where doing their level best, playing "Soldiers of the Queen", and then "Rule Britannia" etc, I dont think the harbour of Albany had ever seen or heard the likes before, the troopship anchored close to us, numbers of the troops remaining up the rigging for some time, The next morning the "Royal Party" left the ship and proceeded by train to "Freemantle", and we proceeded to take in 450 tons of coal, and we had finished and was under weigh by seven in the morning bound for "Freemantle" arriving there in very fine weather the 23rd of July.

Western Australia

Freemuntle
&
Perth

Most of our time here was spent in getting 1450 tons of coal into our bunkers after which I managed to run up to "Perth" for a few hours, and it a flourishing city well decorated and the arches where some of the best we had yet seen, and the people just as loyal and enthuastic as ever, but the great event was. "The farewell to Australia" Like "Adelaide" the people began to assemble early in the morning; but in much larger numbers by eleven in the forenoon a dense mass of people had monopolised every inch of space on the

THE GOLD ARCH AT PERTH. THE GILDED PORTIONS REPRESENTED THE TOTAL AMOUNT, IN CUBIC INCHES OF GOLD, TAKEN OUT, SINCE ITS DISCOVERY

wharf, opposite the ship a large gallery had been erected, this was packed with ticket holders and at one end of it was two or three thousand school children each with a "National flag," The arrival of the "Duke and Duchess" was first heralded by the thunder of the "Royal Arthur's" guns, saluting. The "Royal Party" landed by entering the "Ophir" the starboard side, and then walking across the ship and out the opposite side, on to the wharf; their appearance being the signal for a tremendous outburst of cheering on the part of the multitude; the "Duke and Duchess" acknowledging it by bowing to the right and left; After shaking hands etc, with all the big men of the town, they walked up to where the children sat; As their "Royal Highnesses" approached, they burst into a shrill cheer waving their flags franticly, but after no little difficulty the teachers restored order, and as the band played the "King"; the children burst forth into song, singing the first two verses of The "National Anthem", and then began to cheer and wave their flags; again their childish voices rising high above the hoarser and deeper cheers of the crowd; It was an impressive sight and one not easily forgotten. The "Duke and Duchess" now walked back to where a canopy had been erected over the head of the first pile; A model of a pile driver, with a bottle of champagne for the driver, was also rigged up. The "Duchess" was now asked to step up on the platform and christen the pier, first an address was red out explaining all about the pier, the amount of wood, ect, the "President" of the committe now gave the "Duchess" a pair of scissors, with which she cut the cord suspending the bottle; at the same time naming the pier "Victoria" The bottle fell and smashed on the head of the pile, whilst the cheers of the people broke out afresh; Their "Royal Highnesses" now walked back to where all the notables where gathered, and one by one they wished them all good by, shaking hands with each one individually; and as their "Royal Highnesses" turned to proceed on board, the cheering

was deffening

Farewell
to
Australasia

26th July .01.

A farewell luncheon was held on board
between the hours of one and two, after which
all guests left the ship, "Lady Lawley" had
tears in her eyes, as her little son remained
on board, to take passage to "England," The
sailors where now very busy casting off
the large steel hawsers, which secured the
"Ophir" to the pier. As soon as the tugs started
to haul us away from shore, the pent up
feelings of the people ashore, could not be

restrained longer, and a tremendous cheer went upwards, whilst the bands played the "King", Our band now began to play "For-auld-lang-syne", which set all the people singing, At the conclusion the cheering was louder than ever; "Rule Britannia"

THE ROYAL ARTHUR'S FAREWELL

came next. and then "Home sweet Home", The huge crowds became very quiet as this was played; except for one man who stood on his head. We now began to move slowly down the harbour, their "Royal Highnesses" on the bridge, The "Duke" now turned to the crew of the "Ophir" and cried; three cheers for

"Australia", which we gave right heartily, and set the hundreds of thousands ashore. cheering again, As we passed slowly down the harbour by steamers and sailing ships, each one a mass of human beings, the noise was deffening, hooters whistle's, bells, each vied with one another in making the most noise; but as we increased our speed, we soon left everything far astern, and the "Royal Arthur", came up astern to act as escort In a few hours "Australia" was a thin grey line astern; gradually getting more indistinct untill it dissapeared altogether, yes the land where we had spent many an happy hour was gone. but not forgotten. That night the "Royal Arthur" wished us fare well, by firing rockets and displaying on her side the word farewell in electric lights, and she made a very pretty picture indeed. In the middle watch searchlights flashed on the sky line miles ahead, which afterwards turned out to be the "Juno" signaling

Our next place of call was "Mauritius," the journey occupied nine days in which some interesting events took place. In the first place some sports took place and prizes, such as watches, knives, pencil cases, clocks, etc, where given by the "Duke & Duchess" it went off very well indeed; and Their "Royal Highnesses" were exceedingly amused at the capers of the men, as the ship was rolling and pitching somewhat

THE
WHEELBARROW
RACE
-
SHIPS SPORTS
-

The Tug of war and most of the other events were won by the bluejackets. The next day the whole of the crew of the "Ophir" mustered on the boat deck, which had been made a bit ship shape. The Duke and Duchess, with their Suite, then arrived and took their positions in the center of the group; and the ships photographer took about four or five negetaves; and then we all dispersed. It pleases me here to state that the "Duke" said he would like to see this Log Book and I at once complied with his request; and when it was returned, they sent word that they where delighted with it, and would like to see it again at a later date, We sighted the "St George" the next day, and the following sunday afternoon; about four o.clock we ran into "Mauritius", and dropped both anchors making our stern fast to a buoy.

Mauritius

Here we found an old friend "H.M.S. Highflier."
and with her "H.M.S. Cossack." Their "Royal
Highnesses" and Suite, went ashore the next day;
but I know nothing of what happened an shore
as non of the crew were allowed leave; because
of the plague. Like "Freemantle" our time here
was nearly all occupied coaling ship, We had
about 250 men to assist us, from the "Highflier"
and "Cossack," and then it took us considerably
more than twenty four hours to take in one
thousand one hundred tons, these men where
victualed on board of us; and seemed surprised
when they got sausages and mash for breakfast.
On the 8th of August, their "Royal Highnesses"
returned to the ship. and after luncheon, we got
up anchors. and after all guests had gone over
the side, we swung round, and admidst the cheers
of the "Highflier; Cossack;" and the soldiers on
shore, we slowly steamed away, increasing our

speed, untill our usuall forteen knots was reached, with our escort in their usual positions "Durban" was our next port of call, and as the weather was exceedingly fine we expected to make a good run of it. But our expectations where doomed to be disappointed, as it soon got rough, and the "St George" made a very

THE
St GEORGE
MAKING A BAD PASSAGE

bad passage of it, pitching to an alarming extent and taking tons of water on her fo-castle, which ran off again, as she rose on the next sea, pouring down her sides like a waterfall. On the evening of the 12th Aug a memorable service was held in the grand saloon, in memoriam of the late "Empress Frederick Dowager". The next day we sighted the coast of "Natal" and soon afterwards where anchored off the town of "Durban"

South Africa

Durban

The "Ophir" was too big a ship to cross the bar; so instead of going right inside the harbour we had to content ourselves with staying outside, which was nearly as bad as being at sea, the rollers, rushing in from seaward making it a risky job, in embarking on the splendid tugs, with which the port is well supplied. "Their Royal Highnesses" with part of their suite, left the ship with safety about 11 a,m, on the 13th inst-.

One way of transferring passengers from ships to the tug boats is to hoist them out like merchandise, in large baskets; This method was only used by us once when "Lady Catherine

Coke," The Duke of Roxburg & Mr & Mrs Dereck Keppel came back to the ship. Several large sharks were observed around the ship here. Part of the Cape squadron was here

also to take part in the ceremonies; the S^{nr} "George & Juno" having go on to "Cape Town". The ships here were the "Gibralta" flagship the "Thrush & Dwarfe" gunboats, and the "Barracouta" third class cruiser. "Their Royal Highnesses" returned to the ship, on the 15th Aug and we immediatly got under weigh and escorted

H.M.S. THRUSH.   H.M.S. GIBRALTAR.

by the "Gibralta" turned our ships head for "Cape Town", When leaving two large black fish; a species of whale crossed our bows a few feet away and then commenced to blow, I should put them down as being

between 30 and 40 feet in length. We had very
bad weather as soon as we were well out at sea;
which delayed us considerably, so that we arrived
at Simons Town on Sunday 18th Aug. instead of the
preceeding day

Simonstown & Capetown

H.M.S. PARTRIDGE.

Simons Bay.

As we proceeded up the bay, we saw on our
left hand a Boer prisoners camp, it was early
morn and but few Boer's were astir, but the
ever watchfull sentries could be plainly seen
and as they turned on their beat, something shone
forth like burnished silver over each mans shoulder

H.M.S.TERPICHORE

H.M.S.NAIAD

H.M.S.MONARCH

H.M.S.FORTE.

It was the sun shining on the blades of fixed bayonets. In Simons bay we found the following British men-of-war; the "Monarch, Forte, Partridge, Terpischore, Naide," and the prison ship "Penelope," together with our old escort. the "St George and Juno" We occupied the "Monarchs" moorings, Their Royal Highnesses" did not land till monday; As they where pulled ashore all the ships saluted, The noise of the guns echoing and re echoing amongst the lofty hills, which surround

PRISON SHIP

the town; As their "Royal Highnesses" landed an interesting affair was, that they where drawn in their carriage by bluejackets, instead of horses, all the way to the station. The

"Duke & Duchess," with their suite at once entrained and proceeded to "Capetown", The "St. George" and "Juno," also weighed anchor, and left for "Capetown", but we immediately prepared for coaling, and by mid day we, together with some three hundred men from the "Gibraltar Forte Partridge Monarch Naiade Terpischore", and some

seedy boys or blacks, where up to our eyes in coal dust, We finished coaling about midnight on Tuesday having got in about twelve hundred tons, the following day

we had our hands full cleaning ship, but we got over it all right, and in the evening all the warships gave us a fine display of fireworks

I may here mention that on this day a large number of native chiefs, sent by "His Royal Highness, the Duke", went on board the "Monarch", and there witnessed the firing of the big guns, outrigger charges, submarine mines etc; and they went away, I reckon, more impressed than ever, with the great nation, under whose protection they lived. About midday the following day the 22nd Aug their "Royal Highnesses," embarked, and we at once slipped our moorings, and with the "Naiade and Terpeschore" as escort; we proceeded on our way; the "St George and Juno" had previously received orders to go on to "St Helena". The "Partridge" also came with us, "Admiral Moore" being on board of her. We shaped our course past "Capetown" and in the distance could just make out Table Mountain. The

"Partridge" now turned back, and we increased speed, the high land of the "Cape" rapidly getting lower and more indistinct. But in leaving "South Africa" none of the feelings like we experienced when leaving "Australia" affected us, we had seen so very little of the shore

The last of South Africa

Nothing of any importance took place until the evening of the 26th, when the ship nigger troop gave a concert, and it passed off very well indeed, I may here mention that several entertainment had been given since I mentioned the last one. For some two or

Three months back, the officers had been practicing for a "Nautical Burlesque", and "Chevalier-de-Martino" was painting some scenery for it. About 4·a·m, on the 28th inst,

The "Ophir" ..... Minstrel Troupe

BONES	Interlouctor	Tambo
P.O.II J.Howe	Gr.T.Wright	P.O.I R.Stone.

Accompunist --- F.DANIELS RMLI.

PROGRAMME

OVERTURE	- - - - - - -	TAMBO BONES & PIANO.
OPENING CHORUS	"RING TAILED COON"	TROUPE.
SONG OF THE TOREADOR (FROM CARMEN)		GNR J.COWLING.
COMIC SONG	"I'd like to go halves in that"	P.O.II J.HOWE.
COON SONG	"LILY OF LAGUNA"	P.O.II H.PRICE
SONG	"TAKE A LITTLE PATSY"	GNR - T.WRIGHT
SONG	"THE LOST CHORD"	SGT. S.DACOMBE
SONG and DANCE	"SONG OF IRELAND"	LDG. SEA. A.SILVIE
COMIC SONG	"COUNTY BALL AT SLIGO"	PTE. W.HICKSON
SONG	"JOHNS BULLS LETTER BAG"	BUGLR. H.KIDDLE
SONG	"THE COONS COURTSHIP"	P.O.I R STONE
FINAL CHORUS	"DIXIE'S LAND"	TROUPE

GOD SAVE THE KING

AUGUST 26th 1901

we passed "St Helena", here we where met with the "St George and Juno," who took over their old duty, whilst the "Terpsichore" and "Naiad.", left us to carry out their work all up and down the east and west coast of Africa. I may here mention that on board, was a large number of pets. etc, at every turn one was confronted by cages

containing parrots and paroquets of every shade colour and discription. Also cockatoo's in large numbers, besides quite

a host of smaller birds, We also had a pair of laughing jackasses and a sort of white kywi. In the animal line was a fawn &

SHIPS PETS

a few. oppossum's, including a large white
one; We also had a case of large lizards
but these all died; From time to time in
this book I give illustrations of some
of them; None of the crew was allowed to
have any live stock in the ship; or else the
"Ophir" would have been turned into a floating
menagery. We also had a mail for the

"S.ᵗ George and Juno"

and on the morning

of the 29ᵗʰ we

hove to., and

they lowered

their sea boats, came

DIAMOND
    SPARROW

alongside of us; received

their mail and went back to their respective

ships, whilst we did not wait, but went

full speed ahead, and it took out escort a few hours to catch us up again. It was now getting very warm. Once again we were entering the "Tropical Zone;" Dolphins; also shoales of flying fish, again put in an appearence; but they were

PET FAWN.

of a much larger kind than those we saw

FLYING FISH.

In the Indian Ocean, and thereabouts; during our voyage out to, Australia. On the evening of the 29th; the much talked of Nautical Burlesque came off and was

"A TRAGEDY."
(IN TWO ACTS.)

Who has not read all the details of the shocking outbreak on board H.M.S. "Mantelpiece."

By great good fortune the services of the original actors have been secured, and they are all tamed now, and does it not speak volumes for the system of Naval Discipline, not one of them is dangerous.

Are not their names in history?—so why trouble you with useless recapitulation.

It is entirely due to Mr Wright that the natural tension is somewhat eased by a little music—lest the grim story of the outbreak should cause a breakdown amongst the spectators.

The quarter deck of H.M.S. Mantelpiece has been secured! Can realism be realised more realistically.

GOD SAVE THE KING.

AUGUST. 29th 1901

a complete success; well worth the months of work and practice. The dresses where very good indeed; in fact the whole concern, scenery effects etc, were excellent, Especially when I say that all of it was made out of material that was available on board, Below I give something of what the stage was like, also the principal parts of the play; where petty officer "William Lee" shoots Captain

The play itself, is about a commander who lets his crew do what they like, he is put on half pay; and is substituted by a captain who makes things hum in general; and causes a

mutiny, in which the crew draw lots to shoot the tyrannical skipper, it falls to the lot of the late commander's coxwain, to do the deed; this he successfully accomplishes, and to the crews great joy, their late captain is again put in command. During the jollyfications, at his return, the supposed dead body of the murdered captain comes to life, and he forgives and is forgiven. Tropical showers now began to get very frequent, and our friend "Ventilation", again put in an appearance On sunday 1st sept, in the afternoon, we had a downfall of rain, lasting for two or three hours, it fell so thickly, that our escorts where invisable, though they were steaming pretty close to us. After it was over the sea became very smooth, this was the first smooth sea we have had for some months, and we were enabled now to open our ports on the mess deck, I may mention that only in very calm weather is it possible to do this, or else we should have our messes washed out, but now we were enabled to get a little fresh air

SEAMEN IN TROPICAL & SUB-TROPICAL CLOTHING

and we wanted it I assure you, for our place was like an oven, I give an illustration above, of the sort of clothing wore in the Tropics, of course every one knows that sailors have different clothes for the different climes, but few know the different kinds of rig, at least what they look like. From time to time if time permits I will give the different dresses of the British seaman. We arrived off St. Vincent on the evening of the third of September & there found two warships illuminated which turned out to be our first escort the "Niobe and Diadem", that escorted us from Portsmouth to Gibraltar. We dropped our anchor right midway between these two ships; and the same evening "H.M.S Mantelpiece" was again enacted, as a farewell concert for the "St George and Juno", as their place was to be taken by the more powerfull ships the "Niobe and Diadem". The officers of these ships were also present at the

Diferent Races of People met with During the Tour.

MALTESE LADY

ARAB

MALAY

AUSTRALIAN ABORIGINAL

WEST AFRICAN

AMERICAN INDIAN

entertainment, the officers of the affore said ships, were delighted with it, and were more so afterwards down in the wardroom, the sounds of revelry continuing far into the night. Below I give an appropriate piece of poetry recited during the performance

by
**Prince. Alexandria
of Teck**

Farewell to the "St. George and Juno"

Oh mariniers of England, and those who live at ease,
Remember those two cruisers, which ploughed through many seas.
Steady on either quarter — to guard the White York Rose
Tost and 'twixt it and danger — wher-eir the "Ophir" goes

Twas coaling here, and coaling there, twas coal at every port,
Twas quarantine for weeke and weeks, provisions running short.
And not till St. Helena — did they there harvest reap
The first feed since Port Adelaide — a fine fat frozen sheep

Our sympathies are all with those
Whose escort duties now must close

H. M. S. "JUNO"

St. Vincent.

NAPOLEON'S HILL

Our stay here, as at most of the ports
of call lately, was wholey taken up
coaling ship, We had the assistance
of a large number of bluejackets from
The "Niobe and Juno," a good few from
the first named ship turned out to
be old friends. from "H.M.S.Britannia."
the ship I left when I joined the Ophir,
so I was all right, and so were they, Their
"Royal Highnesses," stayed on board the
"St George" during the day time returning
at night to the "Ophir" to sleep, etc

On the evening following the one we came in, a large troopship crowded with troops came in, and left again about 4 pm the next day. We finished coaling about the same time as she left, and we at once prepared for for sea, and got everything ready for weighing anchor immediatly Their "Royal —

BIRD ISLAND

Highnesses" now returned to the ship and about.6.pm we weighed anchor and proceeded slowly out of harbour passing

PORTUGUESE GUNBOAT

close to the "St. George and Juno," and they manned the ship, and rigging, and gave us three cheers, whilst our band played "Auld-lang-syne," we passed quite close to bird island, an allmost inaccessible rock with a lighthouse perched on top. A Portuguese, gunboat accompanied us out of harbour with manned yards, also our new escort, two ships, that were splendid specimens of "Britain's Naval Might," each one over 12,000 tons displacement, and close on 500 feet in length, with a speed of 22 knots. As we increased our speed the little "Portuguese" gunboat was soon left far astern, when we got fairly out to sea, we found it like a sheet of glass, and

LEAVING "ST. VINCENT."

when night fell it was delightfull;
a cool breeze just put a faint ripple
on the water, and made the air cool
and refreshing; after the heat of the
day, For the weather was quite hot
yet; though we had crossed the line
some considerable time. The next day
the sea was like a sheet of glass, but in
the middle watch the following night,
it began to blow hard, and by daylight
the next day, the sea was, as the saying goes,
mountains high, It soon got so bad that
we had to ease down, It lasted for three
days, and then moderated enough, that
we were able to go ahead again, full speed.
But one thing I could not make out was
although we where steering a northerly

course, the weather still remained the same;
I mean as regards the heat; this may seem
surprising when I say that we were steaming
over three hundred miles each day, Masses

MORE PETS

of seaweed floated past our ship; for
we were in the "Gulf Stream", and a large
number of my ship mates, said that this
gigantic current was the cause of the warm
weather following us, We were now well in
the track of ships, and were continually.

H.M.S."OPHIR."
SEA ROUTINE

A.M.

4 . 0	Call the watch
4 .10	Watch to muster, scrub and wash clothes, except Sundays.
5 . 30	Daymen lash up and stow hammocks, watch fall in, clean boat deck.
6 . 0	Marines and daymen fall in.
6 . 10	Part of ship of watch lash up and stow, cooks, stand easy.
6 . 45	Out pipes, Hands fall in, scrub after part of upper deck.
7 . 30	Sound the charge.
7 . 45	Sound off cooks.
8 . 0	Breakfast, hands to wash.
8 . 35	Up all wet towels on the towel lines.
8 . 40	Out pipes, watch below clean mess deck, watch clean fore part of upper deck
9 . 25	Hands to clean, down all towels.
9 . 40	Stow bags
9 . 45	Cooks watch below clear up mess deck remainder of both watches clear up the upper deck.
9 . 55	Sound the G.
10 . 0	Divisions, etc.
NOON	Sound the charge.
P.M	
12 . 15	Sound off cooks.
12 . 30	Dinner,
1 . 50	Out pipes clear up decks.
2 . 0	Watch fall in, tell off for work.
4 . 15	Out pipes watch fall in clear up decks.
4 . 30	Divisions,
7 . 15	Marines stand by hammocks.
7 . 30	Seamen stand by hammocks.
8 . 0	Clear up decks.
9 . 0	Rounds.
10 . 0	Pipe down.

"INTERJECTION"

It will be noticed by the reader, that very
little is mentioned, about the movements of
their "Royal Highnesses", when ashore, at
the different ports of call.
This is because the writer for several.
reasons did not know himself.
Although we on board the "Ophir" were
interested in the doings of their "Royal
Highnesses"; we had other things to
attend to, for, at most places, when the
"Duke & Duchess" were attending functions
ashore; we were busy, coaling, or cleaning
ship, or carring out work, which as
members of the crew, it was our duty
to do; So all I ask, is, that the reader
of this log, should look on this narative
as just the expression of a lower deck, seaman
on what is an "historic event."

Also the author would like to point out
that the book was written & illustrated.
during the voyage.

passing them, One sailing ship had a narrow escape of being run down by the "Niobe," in the darkness of the night. On the 12th; in the afternoon, there should have been deck sports, but at the last minute, dirty weather again set in, and it had to be postponed All the crew were now well used to the routine, though somewhat different to a man-of-war's, and things were running pretty smoothly. I give the routine on the preceeding page, just as it is posted up in the ship. But there was one thing I dont think we should ever get used to and that was "Old Ventilation", as it was called. Perhaps you dont understand but I will try and explain. On the boat or uppermost deck, where hundreds of cowls or venterlators, as they are called, and sash lights

Now, as long as the weather is fine, venterlators

are trimed to the breeze, and the sashes open;

and all goes well; but at the approach of

rain, the well known cry of the boswains

mate is heard ("Watch close ventilation") and

then the fun starts, all the cowls must be

turned away from the wind, and the sashes

closed down, and they are so numerous

A SMALL
SECTION OF THE
"OPHIRS"
VENTILATON

that one is almost certain to get wet

through, And very often the rain has

passed, and it is fine again, before the ventilation is all closed, it was a scource of continual worry; and this trip we were having a full dose of it, night and day. One more thing I may mention was "Physics or Physical drill," of which we got plenty, and our commander was a

PHYSICAL DRILL

"KNEES" UP

regular school of physical culture, and never seemed so happy, as when he had charge during the drill, Especially when he ordered "knees up," (see illustration). To day a large number of stormy petrels put in an appearance, I think this was

the first time during the voyage that we
have met with these interesting little birds,
They did not come close enough to the ship for
me to take a sketch of them. In the middle watch
the following night a fog
came on, Our commodore
instantly signaled to
take up formation single
line ahead, that is I mean
to our escort, And we got
out fog-bouys, you will
see what I mean, They
are towed astern, and

FOG-BOUYS

the next ship can tell when they are close
upon you, (see illustration) With the fog
came colder weather. On the following
afternoon, we had our deck sports, and
although the entries, were far short of

when we held deck sports, between "Fre
mantle and Mauritius," they went of
just as well, and better prizes were presented
by the "Duke," One of the prize's very much
appreciated was a pipe, with the "Duke of Cornwall
and York's" crest engraved on the silver mount

DECK SPORTS
THE OBSTACLE RACE

Just as the sports were drawing to a finish
a man-of-war was sighted of our port bow
and she turned out to be "H.M.S. Indefatigable"
of the "North America and West Indies —
Squadron," with mails for us. We hove too,
and she lowered a boat, and brought

our mails; together with a pilot to navigate us up the "St Lawrence". The "Niobe and Diadem" also sent their sea boats for mails, As soon as this little transaction was over; she went

PICKING Ü
MAILS AT SEA

of in a southerly direction; presumably to "Halifax N.S." By sunset we were entering the gulf of "St Lawrence". About two hours afterwards, a dence fog came on, and we we again repeated the manouvers of the following night; fog-bouys etc, whilst we also used our fog-horn frequently; and

and so did our escort; who were now joined by "H.M.S. Tribune," cruiser, sister ship to the "Indefategable," Extra look outs were also posted on the fo-castle; and water tight doors closed; In fact every thing that could be done, To ensure the safety of the "Ophir". But by two O.clock the following day the fog had lifted again, so we increased our speed once more. At day break we found a Torpedo boat destroyer off our

"H.M.S." QUAIL.

port quarter, which tured out to be "H.M.S Quail." We had quite an exciting

incident with this little craft later on
in the forenoon; it was about half past nine.
We had despatches for her; and instead of
stopping to give them to her, we rigged out
the lower boom, and made the papers fast to
a rope rove through
a block at the end
of it, for all the
world like a
fishing line. We
were steaming about
fifteen knots at (AN EXCITING MOMENT)
the time, but she came up alongside quite
easily, but a little to far out to reach the
bag; she then made another try, and wether
we moved our helm or not I cant say; but just

as they reached the papers, the destroyer was drawn right under our bows, and as we came together, she heeled over alarmingly; and the ashes came up her funnels in dense clouds, But as you know these boats have an extraordinary speed, so she went full speed ahead, and just managed to slip round the other side of us, missing our stem by a few inches only, Every one was much relieved, when she got clear; as it was a wonder, something more serious did not happen. We were now entering well into the river; but little could be seen, except an occasional glimse of the shore, here and there, as the fog lifted. We were now wearing N° 3.

dress, (serge suits) because of the cold, and the next day we put on extra clothing in the shape of jersey's. On saturday night in the middle watch, we dropped anchor, but as soon as it was daylight, we got under weigh again. We then steamed slowly untill about two O-clock Sunday afternoon; when the fog again enveloped us, and we again anchored,

LANDING RIG. WINTER

Nº 3ªª JERSEYS CUTLASS AND PISTOL

and shortly afterwards got under weigh again, It was getting rather monotonous, we knew that we were surrounded by most

beautifull scenery, and yet could not

see it, Towards evening we passed a

few pecular shaped lighthouses, and

I suppose these put the pilot on the right

course, for we instantly went full

speed ahead again;

and by six O'clock

had again anchored.

All hands were put

over the side to clean

ship, but it came (LIGHTHOUSES
IN THE
S.T LAWRENCE
RIVER)

on to rain, and it

had to be put off

till next morning

The following morn

at daybreak; all hands were busily

employed clearing the ship side. As soon as
this was accomplished, we immediatly got
under weigh, and assisted by a strong current
made rapid progress up the river, passing the
falls of Montmorency on our starboard hand.
Just after ten, A.M, we sighted "Quebec," with
its magnificent hotels perched upon the heights
By half past ten we were safely moored to a buoy,
under the shelter of the Heights of Abraham.

"Quebec."

At Quebec we found the cruisers "Cresent" (flag)

"Psyche," "Pallas," "Proserpine," (British) and a French cruiser, When we arrived the heights, were litterally one mass of human beings, and their numbers were swelled a good deal by the time their "Royal Highnesses" left the ship. The weather was fine, but blowing great guns. All the ships were gay with bunting, only one thing

FRENCH CRUISER D⁞ ESTREES.

out of place, admidst these jollyfications; was the half masted "American flag," In memoriam for the late President. Mc Kinley; which was flown by all the warships present. In the afternoon it became overcast, and shortly afterwards the rain fell in sheets, It was nearly as bad as a tropical shower. I expect it was brought on by the thunder of the saluting guns; that welcomed the "Duke and Duchess" to "Canada." But it was a grand sight to see the quick changes of earth and sky during

this storm, it was like a transformation scene, hills that were green with verdure turned black as night, and the dark troubled waters of the St. Lawrence were turned into a creamy froth by the force of the gale; But it passed quickly, and did good after all, for after it had gone, the wind dropped

which was just what was wanted, as in the
evening, a firework display was to take place
and the fleet to be illuminated. The afforsaid
display was a complete success, one incident
happening, but I dont think any one was
injured, A Tug boat, that was steaming up
and down the river, discharging fireworks, 
had a fire break out in
her chart house, owing
I suppose, to the premature
explosion of some of her
fireworks; she was all
ablaze in an instant, and fireworks flew
about in all directions; to the great danger
of the eyewitnesses; Women screamed, and
men lost their heads, & just as it looked as

PER. MARE   PER TERRAM

ROYAL
MARINE
LIGHT INFANTRY

if a tragedy could not be averted; a couple of
tugs came on the scene and with there steam
hoses, quickly got the fire under control, and
finally put it out altogether. Towards ten O,clock
the sound of singing came from the promenade
up on the heights; it gradually swelled in volume
untill, we, on board the "Ophir," could hear every
word quite, plain They were singing God save the King;
It was good singing, and there must have been
several hundred,s of men and women. Taking
part. The following evening, their "Royal
Highnesses and Suite," came on board to
dine, and all the big nobs were invited; we also
had a repetition of the "firework display."
The people here seem to be very fond of
singing, as, about half past nine, a large

pleasure steamer came off to us; and serenaded the "Duke and Duchess" in fine stile, there must have been two or three hundred trained voices present. The next morning Their "Royal Highnesses" again left the ship. and their stay ashore this time would last close on a month; as they had a long journey before them, across the C.P.R. railway I give a program of the places they visited during their journey across "Canada". The next day we took in five hundred tons of coal, and by eight a,m. the next day was under weigh, and escorted by the "Diadem" only, (the "Niobe" remaining behind to coal) were steaming down the river bound for "Halifax"; there to await the return of their "Royal Highnesses".

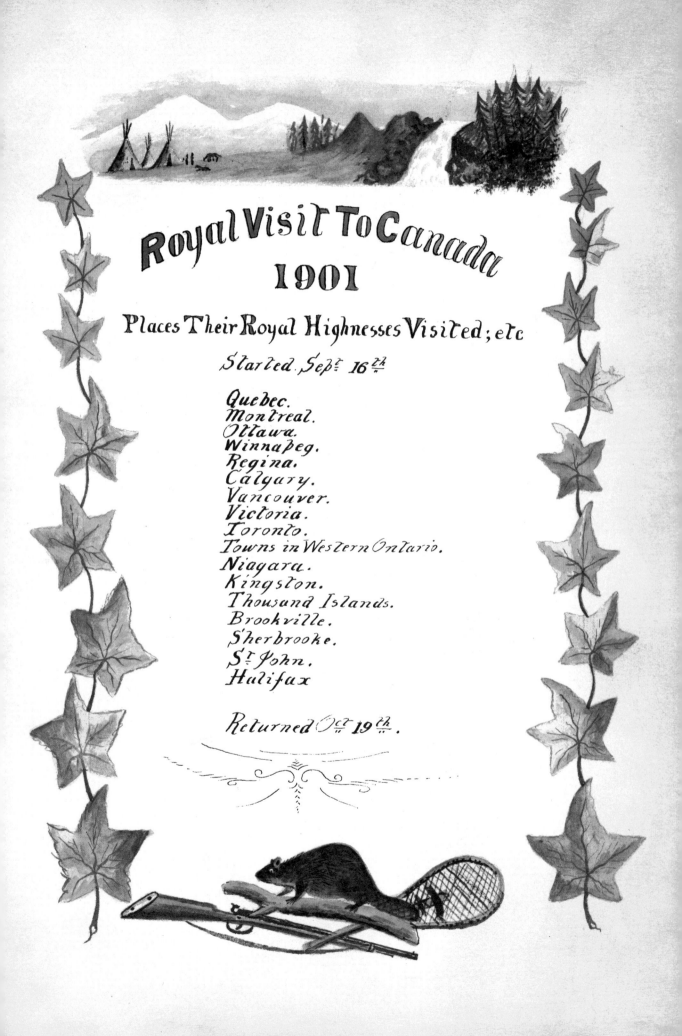

Royal Visit To Canada

1901

Places Their Royal Highnesses Visited; etc

Started Sept 16th

Quebec.
Montreal.
Ottawa.
Winnipeg.
Regina.
Calgary.
Vancouver.
Victoria.
Toronto.
Towns in Western Ontario.
Niagara.
Kingston.
Thousand Islands.
Brookville.
Sherbrooke.
St John.
Halifax

Returned Oct 19th.

from the western shores of Canada. We made
a much better passage down the river
than we did coming up, The weather
remaining clear and bright; and we
were enabled to see some of the beauties
of the river. One thing that struck me
not only at "Quebec" but all up and down
the river, was the amount of churches, the
conspictious part of them being their
spires, some of them boasting three and
one four, there was a grand church; or
cathedral, to every few houses, for
hundreds of miles on both sides of the
river, We passed the island of "Anticosta"
sunday morn; and soon after daybreak

on monday morn, we found ourselves in one of the narrowest and prettiest straits I had ever passed through; and I was sorry when we again passed into the open sea. By seven bells the same afternoon we sighted the two light houses, that mark the entrance to the port of "Halifax." An hour afterwards we were safely moored off a town that; greatly reminded me of one of our large midland manufacturing towns; everything was so black and smoky. The next day a different kind of routine to what we had been used to in the "Ophir" commenced. Of course, as you know we were painted white and our long sea voyages, had left their mark, in the shape of rust; streaks and spots putting in an appearance all over the ship; So this morning each man put on his oldest suit, or refitting rig, as it is called; and armed with either a scraper, chipping hammer, or pot of red lead paint and brush, did his best to remove all

the rust, ready for a through painting; which we were going to receive before their "Royal Highnesses" returned to to the ship. In the morning the "Diadem" went up into an inner bay, for torpedo practice, returning to her anchorage by midday. The next day we still continued scraping, painting etc. On the following morning first thing, we slipped from the buoy, and went straight in dock, and as soon as breakfast was over, all hands armed with scrubbers and scrapers, went into the dock, and standing on floating pontoons gave the bottom of the "Ophir" a thorough cleaning, as the water was pumped out; They say that *matelo's are never so happy as when they are up to their knees in water, and they where very happy this day

(*. French slang word for sailor)

and no mistake; cheers, songs, and yells
came floating up, from the hundred or
more British flat foots, and [‡] leathernecks
as their humor guided them. It was a
private dock   and a large

number of   civilians

gained   admittance

to   have

THE OPHIR IN DOCK AT HALIFAX

[‡] A SAILORS
NAME FOR
MARINES

a look at the "Ophir," but all their interest
was soon centered on the jovial sailors
under her bottom. After dinner we started
painting her bottom with none fouling
composition; and we only finished by
eight O-clock the same evening. We were
out of dock again by half past six next
morning; and about midday they piped
three days general leave for the starboard
watch, (general leave means everyone except
the very worst of characters can go ashore.)
And I assure you kind reader, it would
not do for any nervous person, to accompany
a party of "British Blues" when on "gems".*
Nothing in the way of sport comes amiss

* GENERAL LEAVE

to them; horse riding, cycling, and driving being the favourites. It would do the people at home good, to see a party of bluejackets on horseback, riding full tear, shouting and yelling like red indians. But I am sorry to say that all their pursuits are not so innocent, as those already mentioned, drunkenness being a very predomenent feature during a general leave; but things are changing for the better, the average man finding he is far better off without the drink. I went on leave saturday night, and came off to the ship again monday morning; and I carried on board very plesant recollections of my short stay on shore. I found it a much better place than it looks. One thing about "Halifax" was they knew how to treat a sailor; when he happened to be partaking of a meal. I say for myself that I never had better meals and the charge was very moderate. Of course being one of the ordinaries, I made tracks for some of the low class drinking dens, and met with an agreeable surprise. The neighbourhood was infested with coloured folks, and judge to my surprise when I found them singing just the same coon songs that were so popular at home, And the same old cake walk was very popular there also. But their singing, and dancing, had a certain pecularity about it, that our professionals in the music halls, could never attain to the life. On the Sunday I with several companions, went a lovely walk through forrest and woodland, and altogether, we all had a very good time off it. We returned to the ship next morning, and the port watch then went on their three days leave. On wednesday the 3rd of Oct- we warped the "Ophir," alongside the coaling jetty; and the next morning, as soon as the watch came back off leave, we started to coal ship, with the help of 60 men from the "Diadem and Niobe". There was a large heap of coal, about a hundred yards from the ship; and it had to be carried inboard in small baskets, holding about half.a.hundred weight; it took us three days to take in eighteen hundred tons; But the men where very cheerfull singing the whole day long; We worked from

six in the morning till nine at night. A continual stream of men entered the ship at one gangway and left by another, some carrying their baskets on their heads, some their backs, whilst some carried them under their arms. Now and then the crowd emerging with empty baskets, would form into a body; and then come come charging, and leaping, and yelling like a lot of savages, on to the coal heap, with sticks for spears, and baskets for shields; We finished late saturday night, and cleaned ship sunday morning. On monday we once more moored up to the buoy in the center of the harbour, and commenced painting and scraping as before detailed. Of course everyone that reads, knows all about their "Royal Highnesses." enthusiastic receptions at all the places they visited, and not a small chapter of adventures fell to their lot. We on board the "Ophir," knew no more

about these things than the general public
for our knoledge was gleaned in the same manner
from the Papers

A few objects fast dissapearing from N America

From time to time we were kept in touch
with "their Royal Highnesses," by all sorts of
things. arriving; a "Moose's head" came the
other day; said to have been shot by the

"Duke" in the "North West," A tribe of indians

have pitched their camp on the shore opposite

the ship; and most of them are in full savage

dress, it is a most unusual thing to see them

thus, they have come to see the "Duke" and

must have traveled many hundreds of miles

The "Ophir" now looked a picture indeed, not

a blemish on her snow white side, whilst her masts

and funnels shone like gold in their coating

of buff enamel paint. She looked every inch

a yacht. a credit to the "Nation" to which she

belonged. The "Indefatigable" arrived to day

She had just come from Quebec, having

been tempory repared, after having run

aground, up the "St Lawrence;" close to

"Montreal". Two more ships arrived two
days after, the "Columbine
and Alert"; these ships had
come from the "Newfoundland"
fisheries; Two small
seccond class torpedo boats
were also launched from
the slips, these boats
were to be used for patroll
purposes. when their
"Royal Highnesses" arrived
on board. On the 18th
of Oct, we left
the buoy, and made
fast to the coaling

THE CHILDREN'S WELCOME

Sung by the children in welcoming their Royal Highnesses The
Duke and Duchess of Cornwall and York on the Commons. Halifax N.S.

Wolfe the dauntless hero came
And planted firm Britannia's flag
On Canada's fair domain
Here may it wave our boast and pride
And joined in love together
The Thistle, Shamrock, Rose entwine
The Maple Leaf forever

Chorus
The Maple Leaf our emblem dear.
The Maple Leaf forever.
God save our King and Heaven bless.
The Maple Leaf forever.

On merry England's far famed land
May kind Heaven sweetly smile
God bless old Scotland evermore
And Ireland's emerald isle
Then swell the song both loud and long
Till rock and forrest quiver
God save our King and Heaven Bless
The Maple Leaf for ever

From every heart a welcome springs
Hearts to home and Britain true
Decendants fair of Stately Kings
We pledge our faith to you
God speed you home with breezes kind
His blessing fair you never
God send ye fadeless keep in mind
The Maple Leaf forever

Chorus
The Maple leaf our emblem dear
The Maple leaf for ever
God send ye fadeless keep in mind
The Maple Leaf for ever

Jetty; Here a great transformation had taken place, not a sign of coal, or coal dust

H - M - S . CRESENT

being visable anywhere, new boarding was nailed on the old jetty, and covered with white sand, and all the sheds were painted afresh. The town of "Halifax," was also undergoing a great change, the streets were ablaze with many coloured flags, and bunting. There was no need to erect venetian masts here, as the streets were lined with telegraph poles; that answered the purpose admirably.

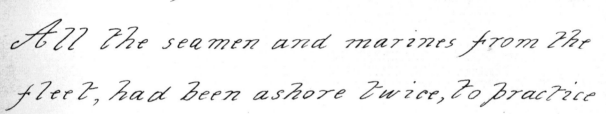

All the seamen and marines from the fleet, had been ashore twice, to practice for the coming review. An exciting boat race took place to day, between the stokers whalers racing crew of the Cresent, and a like crew from one of our escort the Diadem. The Diadem was the challenger, and after a most exciting race of three miles; in which neither boat seemed to gain; the Diadem's won by an extra spurt, when close on the finishing point; by a length and a half. By all accounts; the betting was heavy on both sides, over two hundred dollars being laid down, so our escort would have a nice bit of money to throw away when we arrived in "Merry England." To morrow was the day for the return of "Their Royal Highnesses"

MAKING A PERIQUE OR PLUG OF NAVY TOBACCO

Loyalty of Red Men

Historic gathering of Alberta indians in war paint and feathers to welcome the Duke & Duchess.

WAR CLOUD

HEAD·CHIEFTAIN·

One of the incidents worth mentioning during their "Royal Highnesses" trip across "Canada" was the welcome given by the vast Tribes of "Alberta Indians". The scene was a most remarkable one. The Indians were attired in all the panoply of war paint and feathers. Some of them were almost entirely naked, and had their bodies painted in a most remarkable fashion. One Indian mounted upon a fine horse attracted particular attention. He was painted yellow all over; and his cheeks were daubed with vermilion. His horse was

FALLING. STAR.

streaked with yellow ochre, and decorated in a most striking manner with feathers. Some of the Indians were magnificently attired in furs, plumes, and war feathers, and all were painted in a most fantastic manner. The mounted warriors of the various tribes all armed, formed a semi-gordon in front of the "Royal

Party," and inside it the squaws and papooses occupied a position of advantage. The principal chiefs who presented addresses to his Royal Highness, were signed by "White Pup." "Running Rabbit" and "Iron Shield," head chiefs of the Blackfeet "Crop ear Wolf" and "Day Wolf" head chiefs of the Bloods, "Running Wolf," chief of the "Piegans," "Bulls Head." head chief of the "Sarcees." "Jacob Bears Paw." "John Cheneka," "Jonas Big Stoney" head chiefs of the "Stonies." "Joseph Samson," "Mister Um." head chiefs of the "Crees." May it please your Royal Highness "We, the Blackfoot, Blood, Piegan, Sarcee, Stony, and Cree Indians" "of Southern Alberta," heartilly welcome your "Royal Highness" to the land of our forefathers. For untold generations our tribes hunted the "Bison" on these plains, as a means of subsistence. But the white man came and desired to settle on our hunting grounds, which were already becoming depleted of their large game, principly by the reckless slaughter of the animals south of the boundry line. Consequently about about a quarter of a century ago, we accepted the white mans terms, and surrended our lands by treaty to Her late "Majesty Queen Victoria", whose death we most deeply lament, and of whom you are the illustrious grand-son. On the occasion of this visit, we beg you to convey to your highly-exalted father "King Edward VII". the same expression of devotion to his person, and loyalty to his government, which we promised to his "Royal Mother". The head chiefs of the Indians made the following speeches. "White Pup," head chief of the "Black feet" told their "Royal Highnesses", that he hoped they would live long on this earth, and said this was the first time he had had the priviledge to meet the Queens grandson. "Crop Ear Wolf," head chief of the "Bloods," presented the treaty made 27 years ago, and he said it was first given to "Red Crow", but after three years it was given to him. For 27 years nothing went wrong with them, when "Queen Victoria" was over them. He never calculated on having the ground he was living on made smaller to him. He said that

"Red crow" told him that when the rivers run dry; that is the time they would get nothing more to eat. He trusted their "Royal Highnesses" would take pity on them. The Queen had

WHITE WOLF
INDIAN BRAVE IN WAR PAINT

never had any wrong words with them. "Jonas Big Stoney" one of the head chiefs of the "Stonies" said though art the great son of a great King and that he was great full to the "Great Spirit" for this occasion, and for giving us this brightening day, and all that is peacefull and blessed. The sun now above is breaking through the clouds and gladdening us with its presence. This is the first time I have beheld such a gathering of people mingled together in peace and I am thankfull. "Bull Head" said that all the people round want plenty of grub to make them feel happy when they started for home. He said that was the only thing that kept them alive having plenty to eat

The speeches of the Indians, were delivered in a sort of paraphrased

singsong; at the very pitch of the voices of the speakers

The Dukes reply

His Royal Highness replied to the Indians in the following

Chiefs and men of of the great "Blackfeet" confederation, "Sarcees"

and "Stonies" and "Crees". I have listened with much pleasure and

satisfaction to your loyal words of greeting. And I shall hasten to convey

to my dear father the great "King" your assurances of loyalty and

unswerving devotion to him and his government. I thank you very

much for the welcome you have given me and the "Duchess. in words that

come warm from your hearts. We know of your affection for the beloved

"Queen" who is no more. The great mother who loved you so much, and

whose loss makes your heart bleed, and the tears to fill your eyes

We know this not only from your words, but from the steadfast manner

and loyalty you displayed at the time there was trouble in the land;

and when ill-advised persons sought to sow disaffection amongst you

They failed to do so. The great King my father still

cherishes the remembrance of your fidelity in those days

I am glad to learn of the prosperity that now surrounds the Indian

teepee, and the beautifull and abundant crops, the heards of

cattle, and droves of horses. Those of you who remember the

day the "Government of the Great Mother," first came to you, or

have heard, or have heard with your ears what your fathers have

said, will recollect that your people were often hungry and

wretched, your pipes cold, and your wigwams empty

or melancholy. You know that they did not cry to deaf ears

The "Great Mother" stretched forth her hands to help you

and now those days have passed away, never to return.

You may have wants, such is the lot of everyone on this Earth.

But your requests will allways be patiently listened to by those who have been set by the King amongst you. The Indian is a true man his words are true words, and he never breaks faith And he knows that it is the same with the "Great King." His promises last as long as the sun shall shine and the waters flow. And care will ever be taken over you. I have spoken to you as children of our great "Empire". I know that its flag floats or your tents, and that you wear the Kings colors. I feel that your generous hearts have allready told you, that it no mean thing to belong to such an "Empire" and to share in its glories. As you know it is an "Empire" on which the sun never sets. And I wish to assure you that "His Majesty" your great father, has as much love for you of the setting sun, as of his children of the rising sun. We are glad to have seen you We have come a long way, many thousands of miles across the deep waters and vast prairies to see you We will allways remember this day with pleasure, and I will only add a prayer, and that prayer, and that prayer is this. With the help of the "Great Spirit". peace, prosperity, contentment and happiness, may be your lot and rest among you allways. "The King" has ordered a silver medal to be struck, to commemorate the day

And one will be presented to each of the "Head Chiefs" which shall allways be kept by him as long as he remains in office and afterwards by his successors. I wish you good bye, and hope you will all return in safety to your homes. After the conclusion of the address by his "Royal Highness," which was interpreted to the Indians, The mounted Indians performed a series of evolutions on horseback which were skilfully executed and picturesque in effect. Then the Indian children sang "God save the King" and the "Royal Party" departed for the train.

"Their "Royal Highnesses" return to the "Ophir"

It was typical Nova Scotia weather, that their Royal Highnesses experienced on their arrival in this province. As the hour of arrival grew nearer the crowds outside the railway depot grew to an enormous proportion. Shortly before 9.15. a.m. the Viceregal Train was reported approaching, and before the scheduled time the train pulled up at the platform. The approach of the "Royal Train" caused a buzz of excitement, as it became known, ending in cheering from the immence concourse, as the rumble of wheels was heard outside, As soon as the train came to a standstill members of the "Royal Party" began to alight, and were welcomed by the "Leiutenant-Governor" and others awaiting their arrival. From the landing platform the "Royal party" proceeded to the platform prepared for the presentation of addresses; being received with prolonged cheering by the immence crowd, At the conclusion of the ceremony their "Royal Highnesses" decended from the platform and entered their carriage, and the "Royal proccession moved

forward. deffening cheers coming from every
quarter, all along the route, untill they
entered "H. M. Dockyard," right along the
roadway from the dockyard to the "Ophir"
was two lines of Bluejackets one on either
side with drawn cutlass. It was a quiet affair
coming on board; a naval guard of honour was
drawn up on the jetty, but the multitudes
saw nothing of the embarkation, In the afternoon
the "Royal party" again left the ship. The
"Duke" on horseback in the uniform of the
"7th Fusiliers" and the "Duchess" in her carriage
they went to attend a review in which
over "5.000 Bluejacket Marines and Soldiers"
were present. The next day sunday just
after church the whole of the crew went

out on the jetty and had their photo's taken with their "Royal Highnesses" and suite in the foreground In the afternoon a state luncheon was held on Board

The following day was bleak, cold, and dull, the 21st Oct and the day of our departure from Canada, It was about 9-30 a.m. when we let go our hawsers and the fleet began to slew, bows down the harbour. There were not many people, but they were very enthusiastic and our band played the "Maple Leaf" and et several Just as we commenced to move, the air was filled with falling snow, and it continued, untill we were well out to sea, The fleet now saluted. Turned round and went back with the exception of the "Niobe, Diaden, Cresent & Proserpine"

LEAVING HALIFAX N.S.

These ships then took up their positions; the "Cresent" a good distance ahead of us, the "Niobe and Diadem," on either side, and the "Proserpine" well astern. The reason of this was, icebergs, dense fogs, etc were common in these latitudes, and being surrounded thus by ships, it was impossible to meet any danger, without timely warning. The weather now was very cold, and snow kept falling from time, to time. At daybreak on the morning of the 23rd Oct we were in sight of "Newfoundland"

St. Johns.
Newfoundland

We entered St. Johns, about 7 a.m. passing in between two high rocky headlands. It was an extremely narrow entrance, and very skillfull navigation was required. On our right as we passed in, these words, high upon the face of the cliff, in large white letters, were very conspicious ("Welcome to Terra Nova"). Inside we found "St Johns" to be a large and flourishing town with several fine buildings; Here we met with "H.M.S. Charybdis"; and what we thought

WELCOME TO TERRA NOVA

to be more men-of-war, turned out to be steam trawlers, with checkered sides and yellow funnels there was also many hundreds of fishing boats. whalers sealers and cod boats. "Their Royal

High nesses" did

not go ashore til

the next day, the

24ᵗʰ The decorations etc were

extremely good, taking into

consideration the

elements, which were

cold wet and windy; There were several fine arches

and the poorest houses had their show of decoration

"The Royal Party"

was very well receiv

on landing; The people

cheering themselves

A PRESENT FROM
NEWFOUNDLAND
TO
THE YOUNG PRINCE EDWARD

hoarse. Amongst the presents received by their

"Royal Highnesses," was a "Newfoundland" dog harnessed

to a small mailcart. The dog was a beauty, and

though only nine months old, was nearly as strong

as a man. This present was for young "Prince Edward"

their "Royal Highnesses" eldest son. Both nights during

their stay here; the town and fleet illuminated, there

was also firework displays, whilst high upon

the rocky mounts, burnt huge bonfires. The "Royal

Party" did not stay ashore very long, as the weather

was wretched. The next morning about 6 O-clock

the "Cresent. Niobe and Diadem" weighed anchor and

one by one, proceeded out to sea. Below I give some

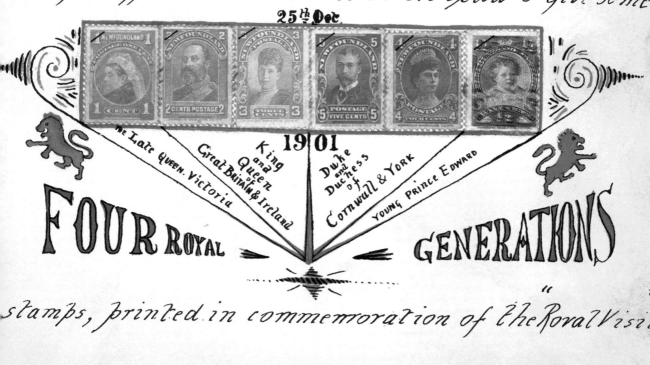

stamps, printed in commemoration of "the Royal Visit"

Homeward Bound.

The Cresent bidding us farewell with her 6in Guns

It was about 7. a.m, by the time we cast off from the jetty, and we immediatly steamed out to sea, and picked up with our escort; "The Cresent" steaming ahead of us. About 9. am she steamed round in a circle, and came close up along side of us, her crew manned ship and afterwards manned the rigging. Her band then played the "King," and then "Home sweet home," "Auld lang syne", and "Rolling Home to merry England." Her crew mean while giving us three hearty cheers which we returned. She then began to shear off, and drop astern; saluting at the same time with her 6" quick firing guns. We at once went full speed ahead and soon the "Cresent" was a speck on the horizon. The "Diadem" was ordered to go on ahead, and report any ships etc. A cold wet wind was blowing from the N.E., and about midnight

she reported an iceberge off our port bow, and soon afterwards played her searchlight full upon it. We passed it quite close, by its appearance it looked as if it had been floating about some time the sides of it being quite smooth. It was a beautifull sight but a terrible danger to shipping, especially in misty or foggy weather, but it took but a short time to dissappear from view at the rate we were traveling. All the men were in great glee at the prospect of soon being in "Old England" once more. "Portsmouth" was looked forward to with more interest than any place we had been to yet; and sea songs, mostly about going home, were the order of the day, and night. "Rolling Home to Merry England," being the favourite. And without a doubt we were "rolling home, for with an heavy sea on our beam, we were. rolling to a considerable extent, and continued to do so, for four or five days, untill we arrived off the coast of "Ireland" when the sea subsided a good deal On the morning of the 30th at daybreak we sighted a lot of ships right ahead; which turned out to be the "Channel Squadron," comprising six battle ships, the "Magnificent," (flag) "Majestic," (flag) "Jupiter," "Mars," "Hannibal," and "Prince George," and six cruisers. the "Arrogant," "Furious,"

SIGHTING THE CHANNEL FLEET.

"Hyacinth," "Minerva," and our old escort the "St George and Juno." The battleships being on the right, the cruisers to the left, But they soon formed up and began to steam slowly in the same direction as us; being, some six miles ahead of us. About eight. p.m, they turned about and

H.M.S "MAGNIFICENT"
IN
WAR PAINT
—

came bearing down on us full speed, in two lines, or subdivions line ahead. When they got quite close, one line swung round to starboard and one to port of us; and then forming up into two long lines; one each side flagships leading. Whilst this evolution was being carried out the whole fleet saluted. It was a grand spectacle, and no mistake about it, to see these 15.000 ton fighting machines at play. It does not do to ponder, and think what the scene would look like if these monsters of the deep, was to meet in deadly combat. One thing surprised us all; That was finding the "Magnificent" in full war paint black and grey, and she looked much more formidable than if she was painted in the ordinary Naval colours of black, white, yellow, and red. By eleven, p.m. we were "off Lands End." In the middle watch a stiff head wind sprang up, and soon afterwards it was blowing half a gale. Daylight next morning opened up a splendid scene to view. We were just off "Plymouth." the sea a mass of foam with the force of the wind, and the long line of battleships and cruisers on either side of us, were throwing up sheets of spray right over their funnels. I could make out most of the places, "Salcombe," "Dartmouth," "Torquay," etc, as we made our way up channel, then we lost sight of the

THE OPHIR LEADING THE CHANNEL FLEET.

land again. About 11. a.m. we sight "Portland Bill," our arrangements were to anchor here till the next day, but the weather was so unfavourable that we continued on our way, being joyned by the "Pactolus" second class cruiser with mails About half past 2 in the afternoon we passed the "Needles" "Isle of Wight" and soon afterwards

THE NEEDLES ISLE OF WIGHT.

dropped anchor in comparativly smooth water. In the afternoon about half past four, their "Royal Highnesses" presented the officers and crew with a small medallion as a souvenir of the cruise, the officers being

of gold and the mens silver In the evening

SHOWING BOTH SIDES OF THE MEDAL
PRESENTED TO THE OFFICERS & MEN.
OF
H.M.S. "OPHIR"
BY T.R.H.
DUKE & DUCHESS of CORNWALL & YORK

a dinner party was held on board, Honouring

the officers of the "Channel Fleet." The next

morning about six the whole of the fleet except

the "St George, & Juno", got under weigh, and proceeded

to "Spithead." About 10·30. a.m. the "New Royal

Yacht" accompanied by the "Trinity Yacht Irene"

was seen approaching; the "Royal Yacht" had

the standard flying, showing that Their Majesty's

were on board. As they drew closer we manned

ship, and the "St George and Juno" saluted with

their six inch guns. The "Royal Yacht Victoria"

and Albert came up right abrest of us

and let go her anchor

Home Sweet Home.
the
King and Queen

and the People's welcome home.

THE ROYAL YACHT "VICTORIA & ALBERT"

As soon as possible a steam boat was

lowered from the "Royal Yacht," and was

soon on its way to the "Ophir" with their

"Majesty's" on board. They came up alongside the starboard gangway but the water was so choppy that they could not get aboard; so the "Duke and Duchess," and suite, went down the ladder as far as possible. The King looked very

MAST HEAD FLAGS OF THE "OPHIR"

"PRINCE OF WALES" STANDARD   "TRINITY HOUSE FLAG"

happy indeed, the "Queen" was in the cabin, but he caught her by the arm, and said come out and let them have a look at you. The "Duke's children" were in the boat too, and were eager to catch a glimse of their "Royal Parents," Young Prince Edward came scrambling between the king's legs to have first look. They did not remain alongside long, but waved adieu for the time, and went alongside the "Victoria and Albert," were they had a specially fitted gangway in case of a rough sea. "Commodore Lambton of Ladysmith" fame was in charge of the boat. About two o-clock in the afternoon, we all weighed anchor and with the "Irene" leading and the "S.t George and Juno" bring up the rear we steamed slowly up the "Solent," before long we were surrounded by pleasure boats, steamers, crowded with enthusiastic people, who cheered themselves hoarse, After passing Cowes on the right we came to the fleet anchored in two lines

They saluted us, just before we reached them and each ships company gave us three cheers as we passed them. After passing through the lines, we were hove to for a few minutes to allow the "Royal Yachts" to enter and get berthed first. But we soon went ahead again, the shores on

THE SEARCHLIGHTS OF THE FLEET

both sides of the harbour, were black with people, and despite the strong breeze blowing their cheers could be plainly heard. As we got closer in, the cheering was simply deffening and what with the bands ashore, and our band playing "Home sweet Home," it made a home coming never to be forgotten As we passed in between the narrow entrance to the harbour, with the forts, and houses etc, clothed with people, The fleet saluted; included the old "Victory," and the scores

of steam pleasure boats, kept up a continual din with their hooters. We soon drew up to the same old jetty we left several months back. Here a naval

H.M.S. "VICTORY."

guard was drawn up, and they gave us

three rousing cheers waving their staw hats mean white—. We were soon made fast and the gangway got out, and then as soon as possible the "Dukes" suite ran ashore, and there was much exciting talk and handshakings "Their Royal Highnesses" left the ship soon afterwards, and went aboard the "Victoria and Albert," we did not witness the meeting with the "King, Queen, and children." In the evening a grand dinner was held on board the Kings yacht; the "Ophirs" band attending During the speeches made at dinner the King said this was the happiest day he had spent this year. Right through the

evening up till midnight all men-of-war
illuminated; the "Victory" made a unique
spectacle for between her for and main
mast triced high up, like a sky sign, was
the words ("Welcome home)" in golden electric
lights; a torpedo boat destroyer, berthed

THE "VICTORY"   ILLUMINATED

along side of her, supplied the motor
power. Out at "Spithead" the Channel
Fleet looked grand, clothed with electricity,

Welcome Home.

Welcome and hail! In the moment of meeting,
First on the shore, by the edge of the foam.
Surely the people may offer the greeting,
Welcoming Prince and Princess to their home.

Long was the journey, the whole earth embracing,
Passing through every climate and zone,
Yet it was merely the boundaries tracing,
Marking the Empire that travels alone.

What says the proverb, of him who shall travel?—
He who goes lonely shall travel afar.
Britain perchance may the problem unravel,
Lonely she rides in her conquering car

Allies we need not, and foemen we need not,
Everywhere flutters the flag of our birth
Nations are blind, if the riddle they read not
Britain rides lonely, the Queen of the Earth

Hush for a moment, a father and mother,
Claim the first greeting of daughter and son.
Then the whole Nation shall offer another,
Joyful to know, that the journey is done

Yet it was only the lord of the manor,
Sending his heir, to look round the estate.
Starting from home with the family banner,
Welcomed to day once again at the gate.
—— " ——

Only his land is an Empire extending,
Over the world, and maintaining her sway
Eastward and westward in glory unending,
Sunlit through every hour of the day
—— " ——

Home from the tropical haunts of the Tiger,
Home from the regions of iceberg and snow.
Home from the lands, where the Nile and the Niger,
Form but new paths, where our sailors must go.
—— " ——

Home from the Commonwealth proud of her glory,
Land of the duckbill, dingo, kangaroo.
Latest to add, to the Empires great story
One more new chapter, as strange as its true
—— " ——

Home then at last! Now the journey is ended
Gladly we welcome you back to the shore
After a run through an empire so splendid
All that we ask is to leave us no more
—— " ——

Hopeful we greet you our prayers addressing,
To him who rules over all things above.
May he upon you, pour every Blessing,
Guiding you ever in wisdom and love.

After their return The "Duke & Duchess."
received the titles of "Prince & Princess of Wales"
and they were entertained by the "Lord Mayor
of London", at a banquet in the Guildhall
on the "5th December 1901."
The following is taken from a speech made
by his "Royal Highness". It may interest
you to know that although. we travelled over
forty five thousand miles; (With the exception of
Port Said) we never set foot on any land where
the "Union Jack" did not wave. (Loud & prolonged applause
If I were asked to specify any particular

impression derived from our journey. I should
at once place before all others that of loyalty
to the "Crown", and attatchment to the old
country, by our "Colonists" It was indeed touch:
to hear the invariable references to "Home"
Even from the lips of those who never had be:,
nor were ever likely to be in these islands.
In this loyalty, lies the strength of a true
and living membership, in the great & gloriou
"British Empire"

THE ROYAL TOUR
1901

GIBRALTAR
MALTA
ADEN
EGYPT
INDIA
CEYLON
SINGAPORE
AUSTRALIA
NEW
ZEALAND
TASMANIA
MAURITIUS

SOUTH
AFRICA
ST.HELENA
ASCENCION
QUEBEC
ACROSS
CANADA
VANCOUVER
NIAGARA
FALLS
NEW
FOUNDLAND

'H.M.R.Y. OPHIR.'
WITH ESCORT: NIOBE & DIADEM
DISTANCE COVERED OVER 50 THOUSAND MLS